PIANO/VOCAL/GUITAR

W9-BAD-865

Contemporary Disney

Disney and Disney/PIXAR characters and artwork © Disney Enterprises, Inc.

ISBN 978-0-634-02830-4

Walt Disney Music Company
Wonderland Music Company, Inc.

DISTRIBUTED BY

HAL•LEONARD®
CORPORATION

7777 W. BLUEMOUND RD. P.O. BOX 13819 MILWAUKEE, WI 53213

In Australia Contact:
Hal Leonard Australia Pty. Ltd.
4 Lentara Court
Cheltenham, Victoria, 3192 Australia
Email: ausadmin@halleonard.com.au

Visit Hal Leonard Online at
www.halleonard.com

BEAUTY AND THE BEAST

from Walt Disney's BEAUTY AND THE BEAST

Lyrics by HOWARD ASHMAN
Music by ALAN MENKEN

Moderately slow

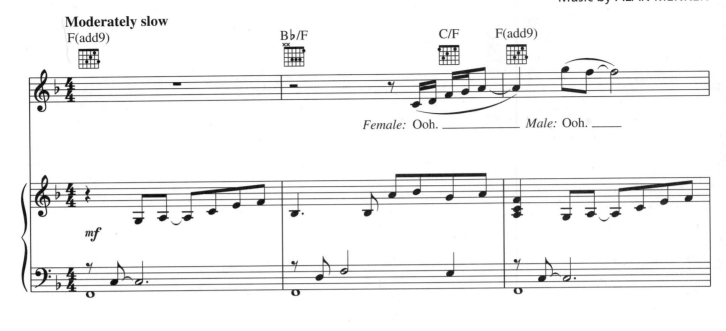

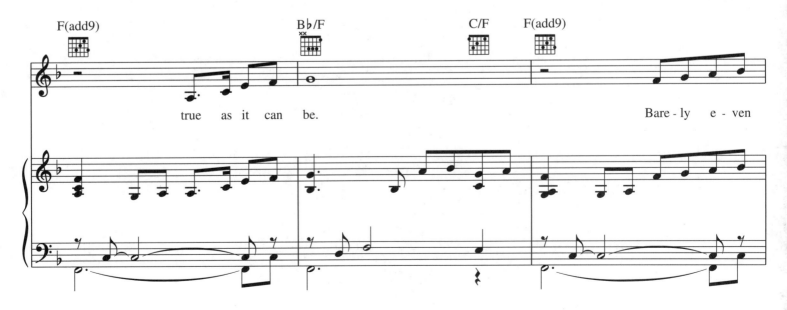

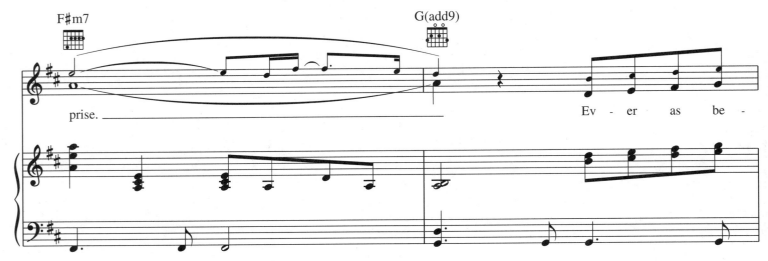

Woo _____ oh. _____

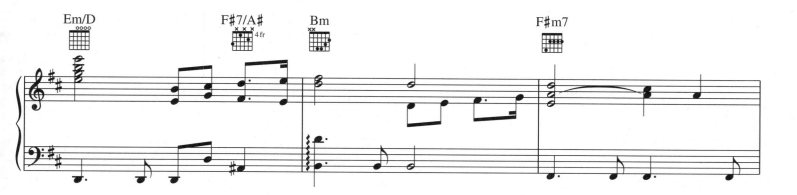

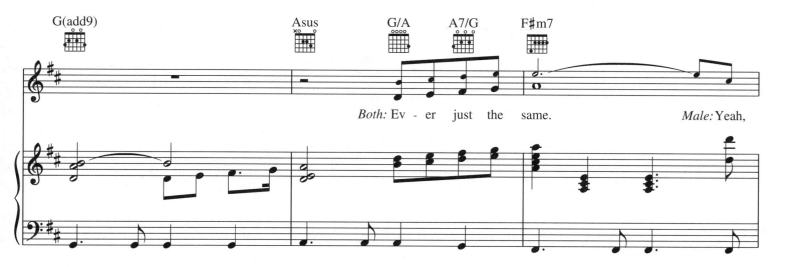

Both: Ev - er just the same. *Male:* Yeah,

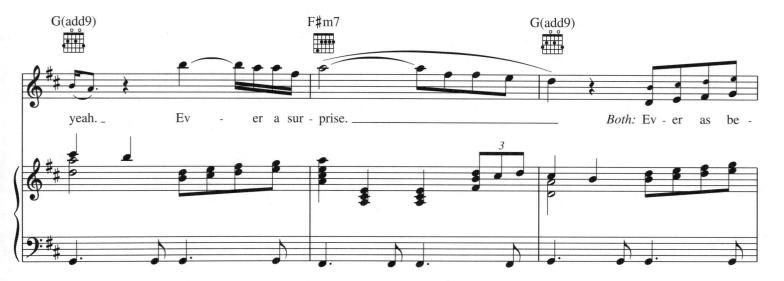

yeah. _ Ev - er a sur - prise. _____ *Both:* Ev - er as be -

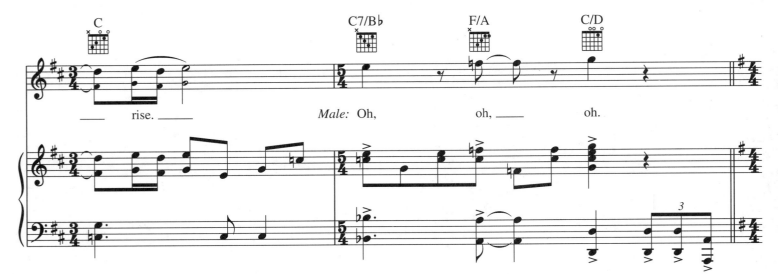

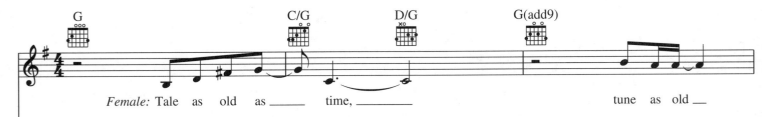

Female: Tale as old as ___ time, *Male:* song as old as ___ rhyme. *Both:* Beau-ty and the ___

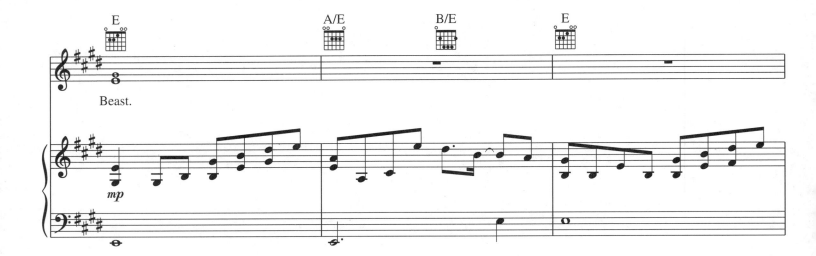

Beast.

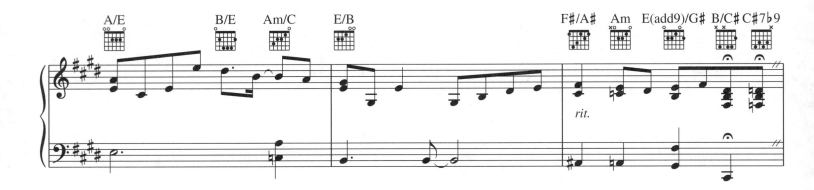

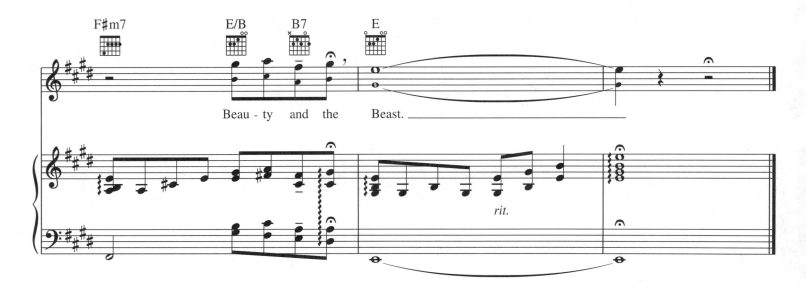

Beau-ty and the Beast. _____

BREAKING FREE

from the Disney Channel Original Movie HIGH SCHOOL MUSICAL

Words and Music by
JAMIE HOUSTON

Moderately

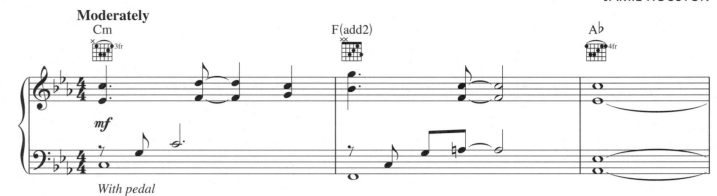

With pedal

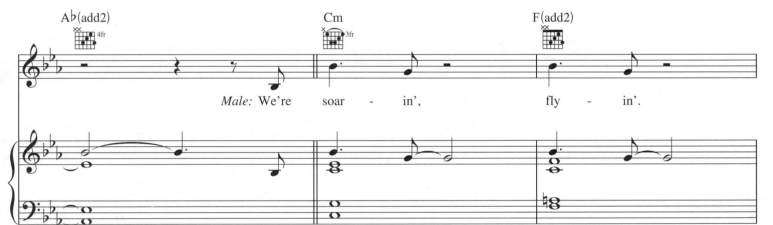

Male: We're soar - in', fly - in'.

There's not a star __ in heav - en that we __ can't reach. __ *Female:* If we're try -

- in', _____ so we're break - in' free.

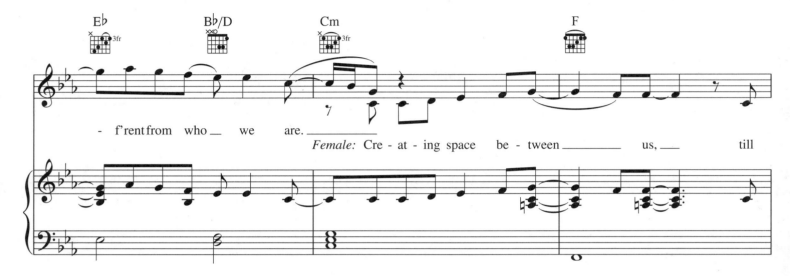

CAN YOU FEEL THE LOVE TONIGHT

from Walt Disney Pictures' THE LION KING

Music by ELTON JOHN
Lyrics by TIM RICE

and it sees __ me through. __ It's e - nough __ for this rest - less war - rior
to the wild __ out - doors __ when the heart __ of this star - crossed voy - ag - er

just to be __ with you. __
beats in time __ with yours. __

And can you feel __ the love __

poco cresc.

__ to - night? __ It is where __ we are. __

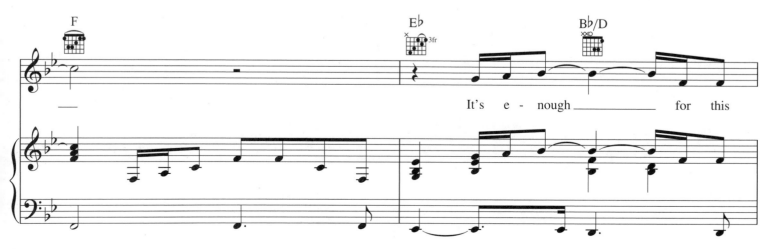

__ It's e - nough _____ for this

wide - eyed___ wan - der - er   that we got this far.___

___   And can   you feel___ the love___

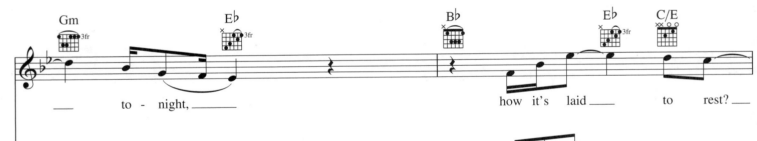

___   to - night,_____   how it's laid___ to rest?___

___   It's e - nough_____ to make

kings ___ and ___ vag - a - bonds ___ be - lieve the ver - y best. ___

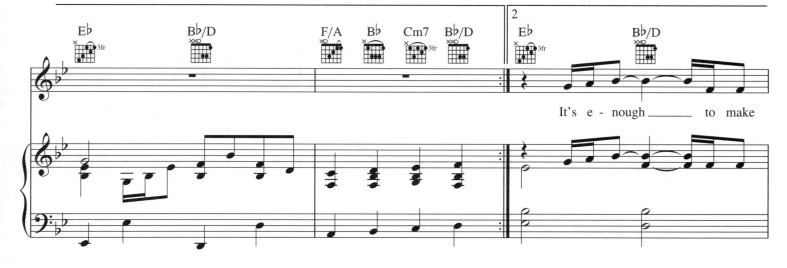

poco dim.

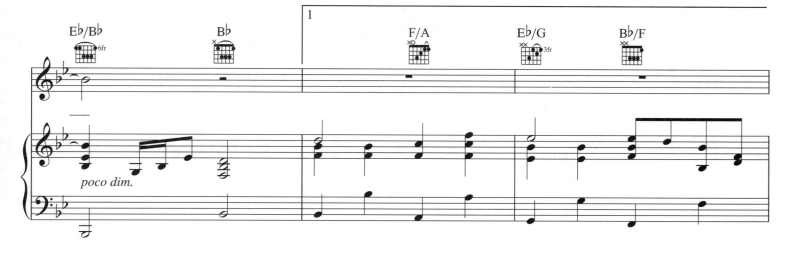

It's e - nough ___ to make

kings ___ and ___ vag - a - bonds ___ be - lieve the ver - y best. ___

molto rit.

COLORS OF THE WIND

(Pop Version)

from Walt Disney's POCAHONTAS
as performed by Vanessa Williams

Music by ALAN MENKEN
Lyrics by STEPHEN SCHWARTZ

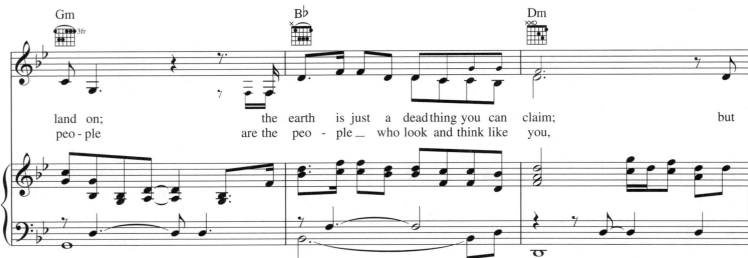

paint with all __ the col-ors of the wind? Can you paint with all __ the col-ors of the

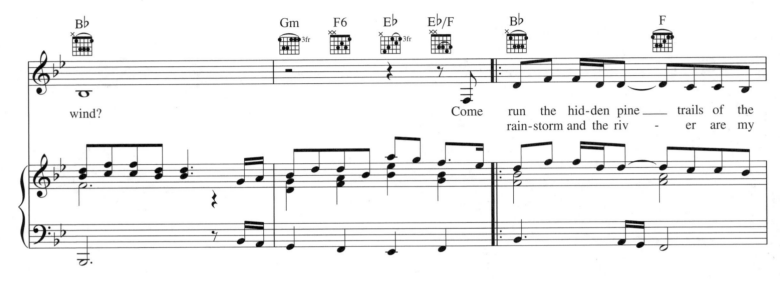

wind? Come run the hid-den pine __ trails of the

rain-storm and the riv __ er are my

for - est, come taste the sun-sweet ber - ries of the earth, come

broth - ers; the her - on and the ot - ter are my friends; and

roll in all __ the rich - es all a - round you, and for once nev-er won-der what they're

we are all __ con-nect-ed to each oth - er in a

D.S. al Coda

worth. The cir-cle in a hoop that nev - er ___ ends. Have you

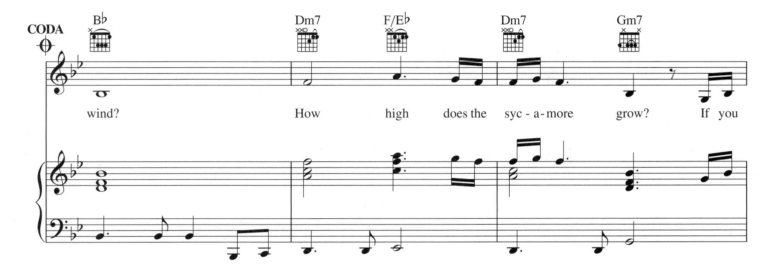

wind? How high does the syc-a-more grow? If you

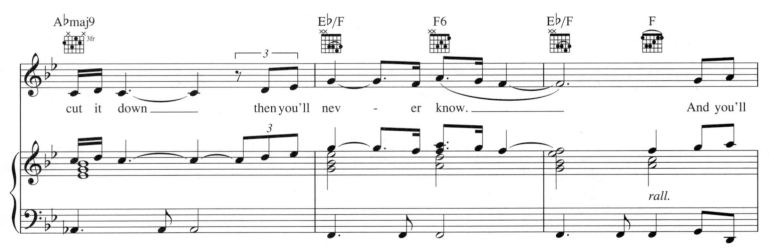

cut it down ___ then you'll nev - er know. ___ And you'll

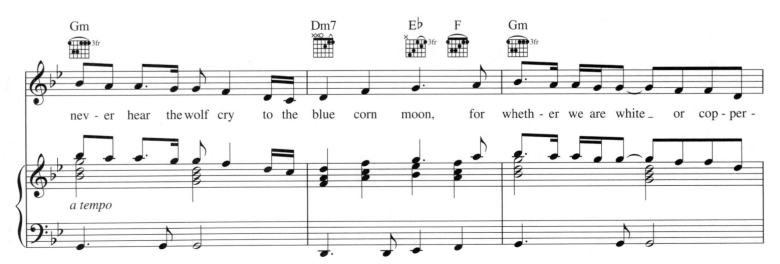

nev - er hear the wolf cry to the blue corn moon, for wheth - er we are white ___ or cop - per -

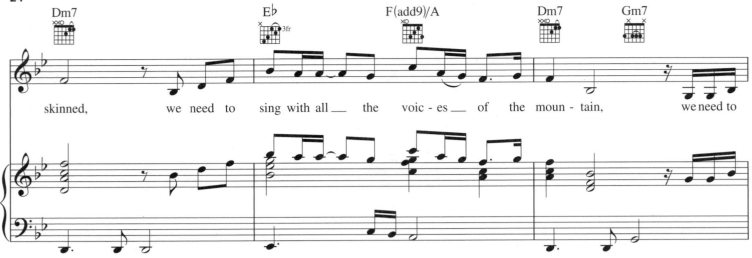

skinned, we need to sing with all __ the voic- es __ of the moun - tain, we need to

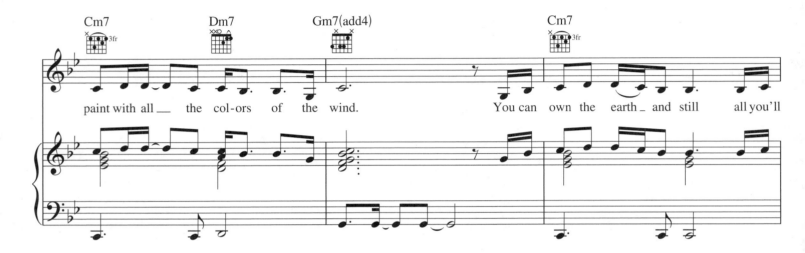

paint with all __ the col-ors of the wind. You can own the earth __ and still all you'll

Freely

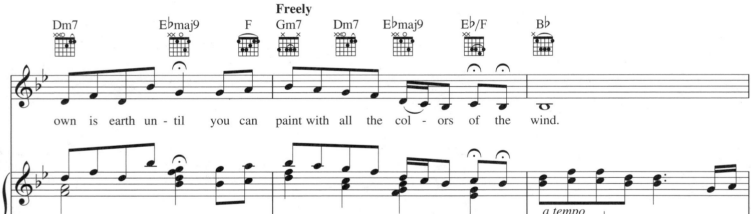

own is earth un - til you can paint with all the col - ors of the wind.

a tempo

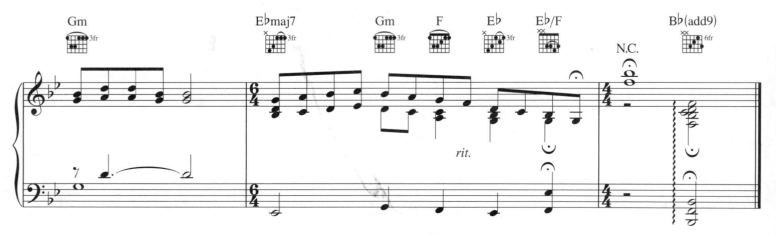

rit.

A CHANGE IN ME

from Walt Disney's BEAUTY AND THE BEAST: THE BROADWAY MUSICAL

Words by TIM RICE
Music by ALAN MENKEN

my child-hood dreams, but I don't mind, _____

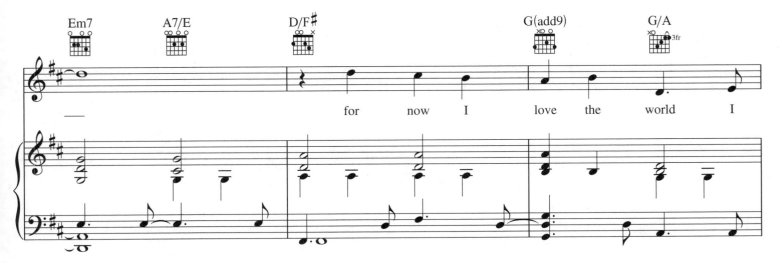

_____ for now I love the world I

D.C. al Coda
(take 2nd ending)

see. _____ No change of heart, a change in

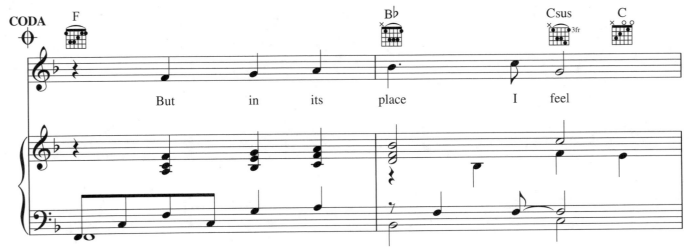

But in its place I feel

a tru-er life be-gin. And it's so good and real,

it must come from with-in. And I, _____

I nev-er thought I'd leave be-hind _____

my child-hood dreams, but I don't mind. _____

CIRCLE OF LIFE
from Walt Disney Pictures' THE LION KING

Music by ELTON JOHN
Lyrics by TIM RICE

Relaxed Pop beat

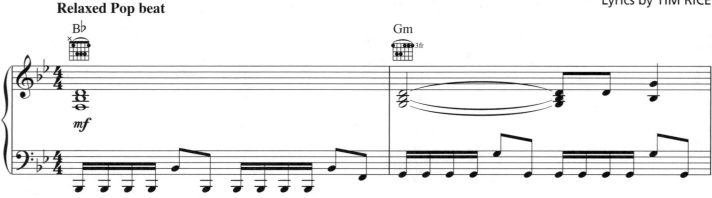

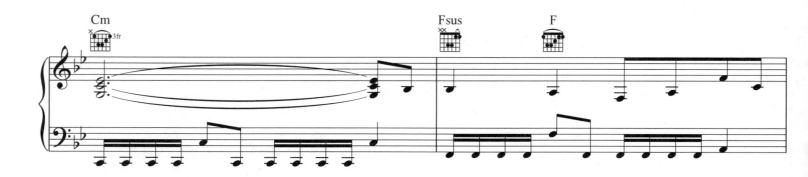

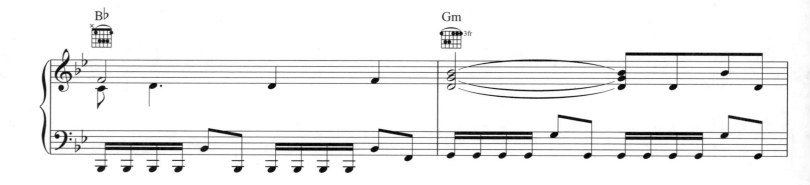

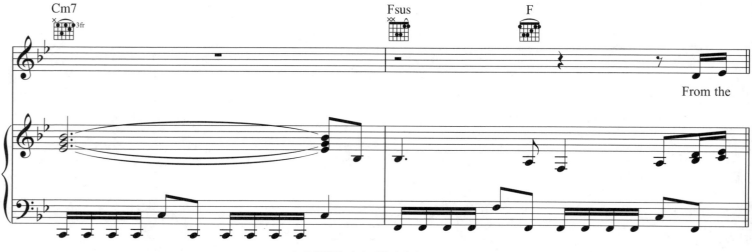

From the

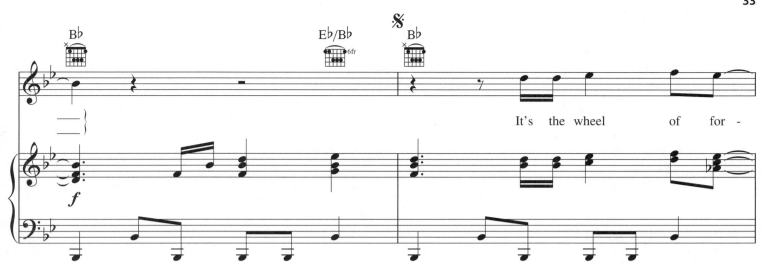

It's the wheel of for-

-tune. It's the leap of faith.

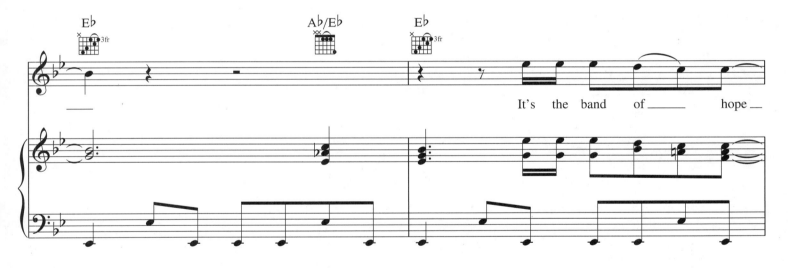

It's the band of ____ hope ____

____ 'til we find _____ our ____ place ____

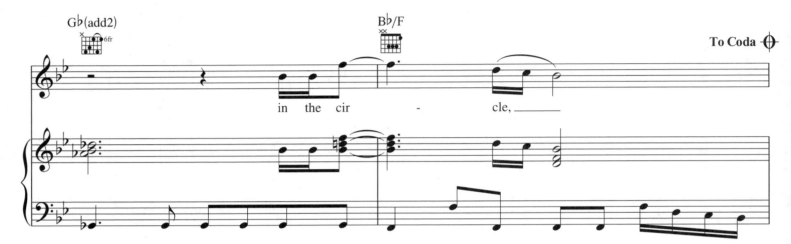

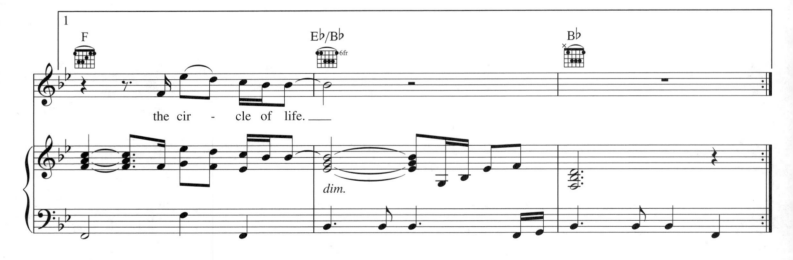

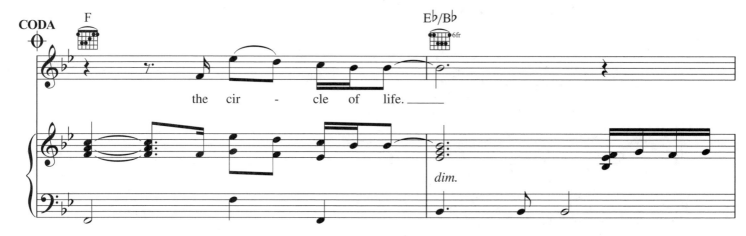

the cir - cle of life. _____

On the path un - wind -

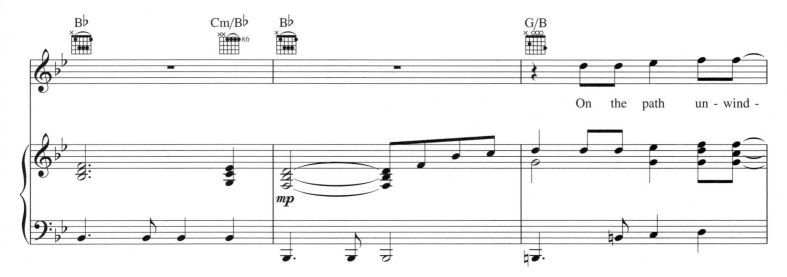

- ing   in the cir - cle, _____

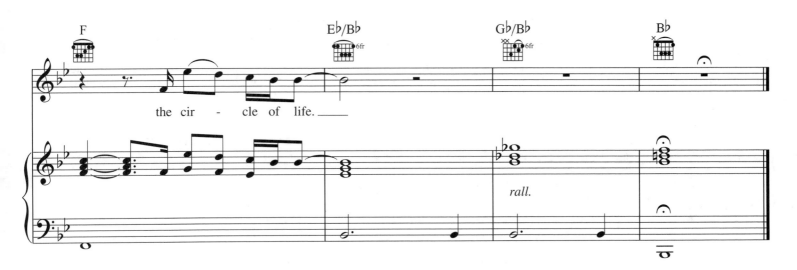

the cir - cle of life. _____

FIND YOURSELF

from the Walt Disney/Pixar film CARS

Words and Music by
BRAD PAISLEY

Moderately slow, in 2

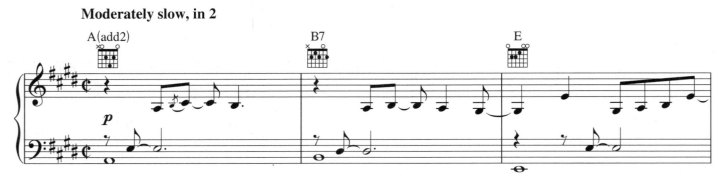

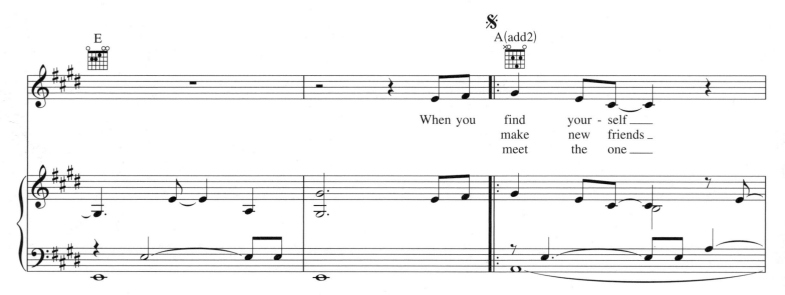

When you   find   your - self ___
make   new   friends ___
meet   the   one ___

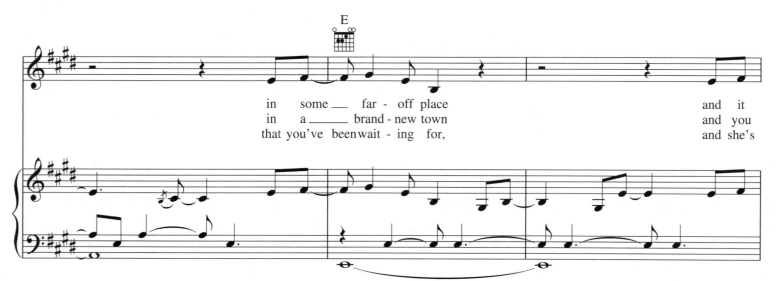

in   some ___ far - off place   and it
in a ____ brand - new town   and you
that you've been wait - ing for,   and she's

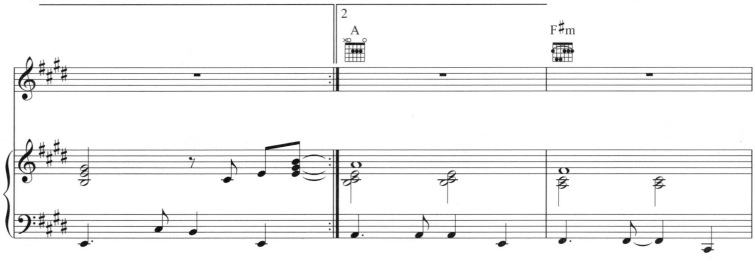

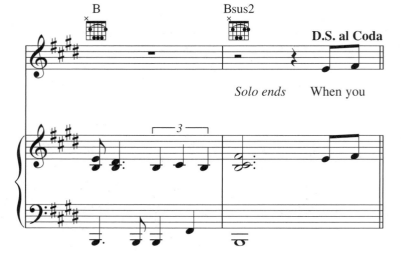

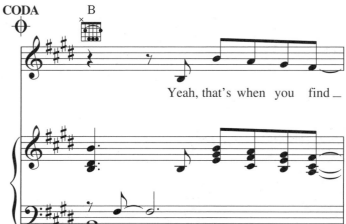

Solo ends   When you

Yeah, that's when you find

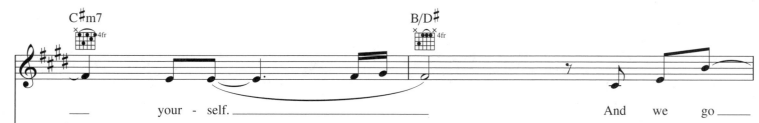

your - self.   And   we   go

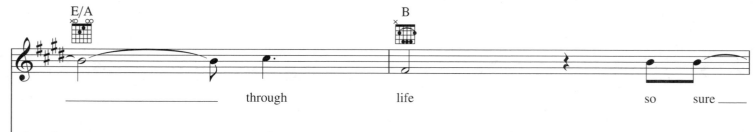

through   life   so   sure

find your-self, __ yeah, that's when you __ find __ your-self.

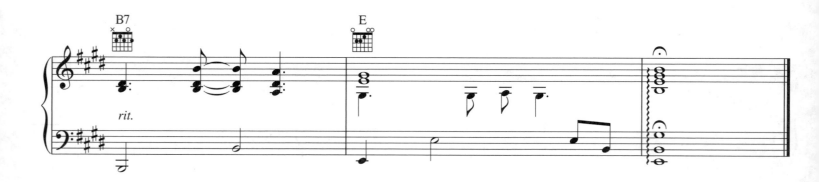

GO THE DISTANCE
from Walt Disney Pictures' HERCULES

Music by ALAN MENKEN
Lyrics by DAVID ZIPPEL

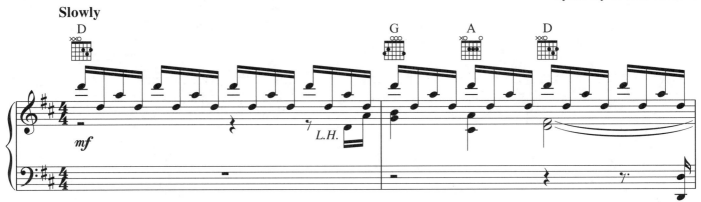

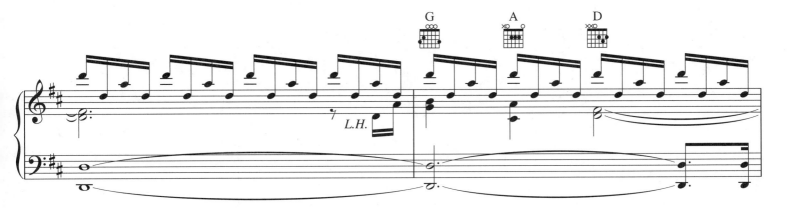

I have of-ten dreamed of a far-off place where a
un-known road to em-brace my fate, though that

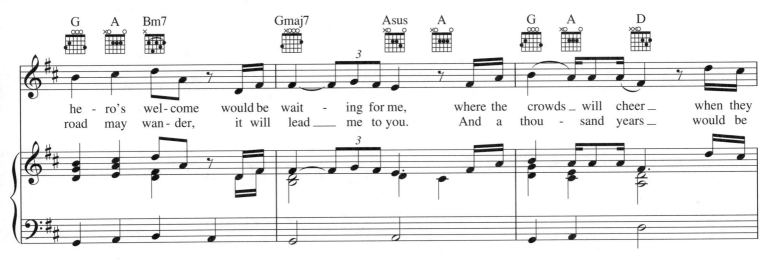

he - ro's wel - come would be wait - ing for me, where the crowds _ will cheer _ when they
road may wan - der, it will lead _ me to you. And a thou - sand years _ would be

see ___ my face, ___ and a voice keeps say - ing this is where I'm meant to be. ___ I'll be
worth ___ the wait. ___ It might take a life - time, but some - how I'll see it through. ___ And I

there some - day. ___ I can go ___ the dis - tance. I will find my way ___
won't look back. ___ I can go ___ the dis - tance. And I'll stay on track. ___ No, I

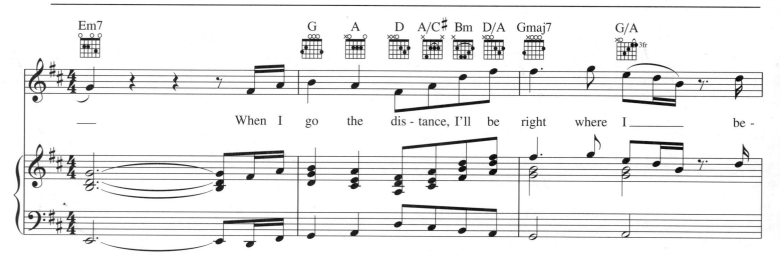

if I can ___ be ___ strong. I know ev - 'ry mile ___ will be worth my while. ___
won't ac - cept ___ de - feat. It's an up - hill slope, ___ but I

When I go the dis - tance, I'll be right where I ___ be -

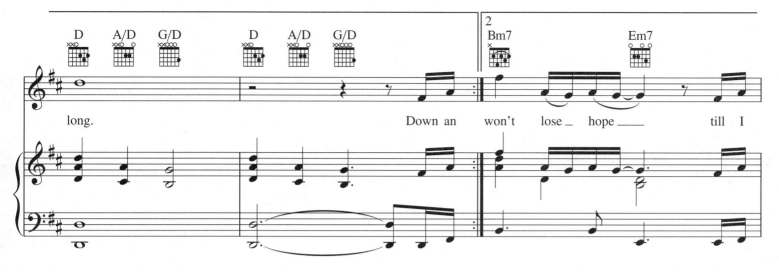

long.

Down an won't lose _ hope ____ till I

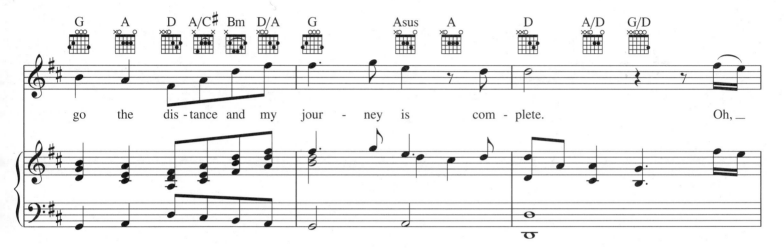

go the dis - tance and my jour - ney is com - plete.

Oh, __

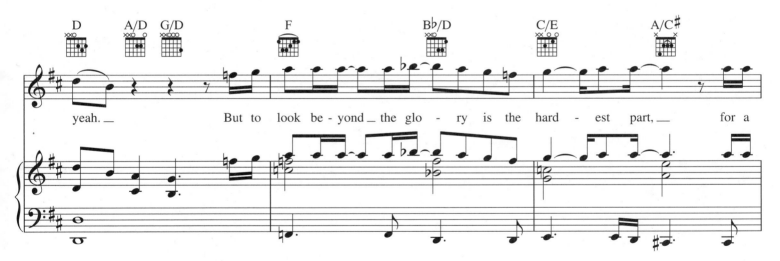

yeah. __ But to look be - yond _ the glo - ry is the hard - est part, __ for a

he - ro's strength _ is meas - ured by his heart.

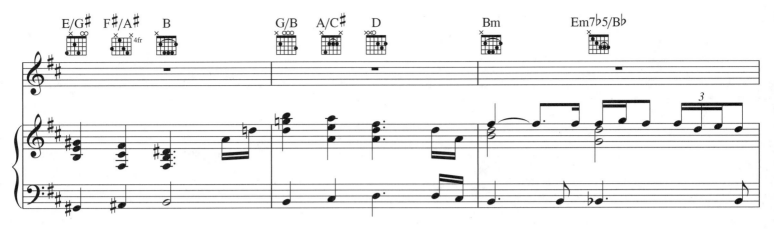

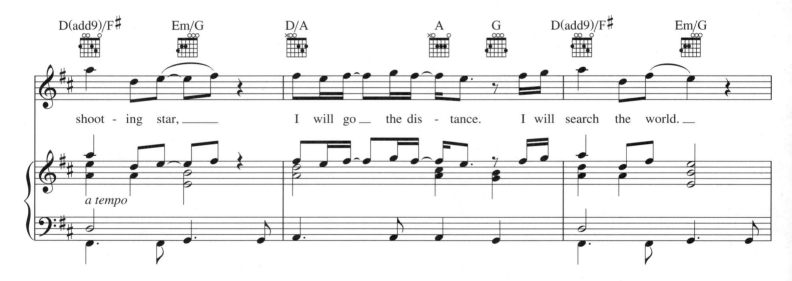

shoot - ing star, _____ I will go _____ the dis - tance. I will search the world. _____

I will face _____ its harms. I _____ don't care how far. _____ I can go the dis - tance till I

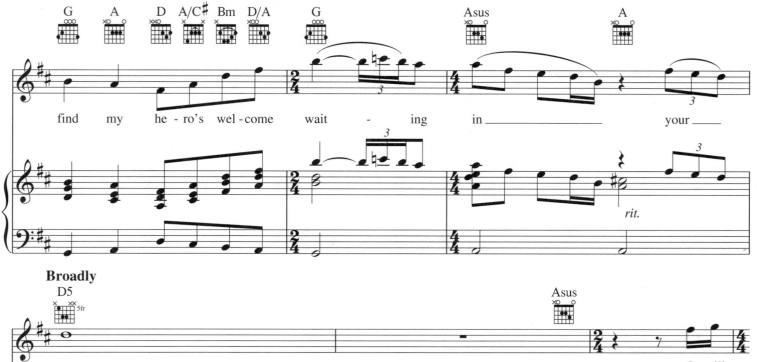

find my he-ro's wel-come wait - ing in _____ your ____

Broadly

arms. I will

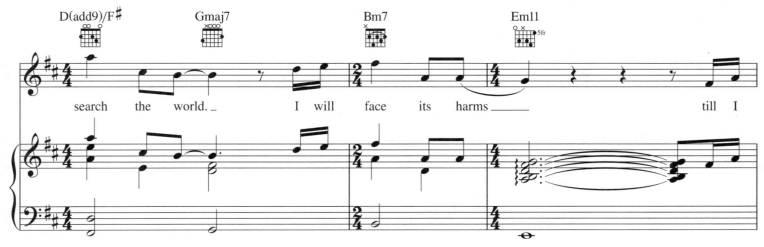

search the world. _ I will face its harms _____ till I

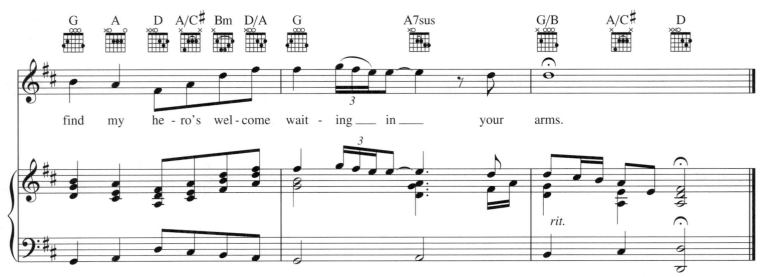

find my he-ro's wel-come wait-ing___ in ___ your arms.

GOD HELP THE OUTCASTS

from Walt Disney's THE HUNCHBACK OF NOTRE DAME

Music by ALAN MENKEN
Lyrics by STEPHEN SCHWARTZ

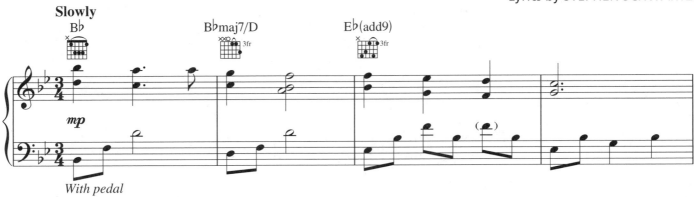

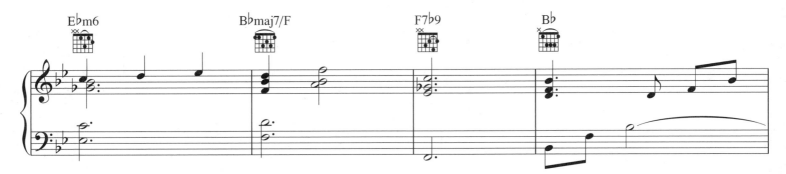

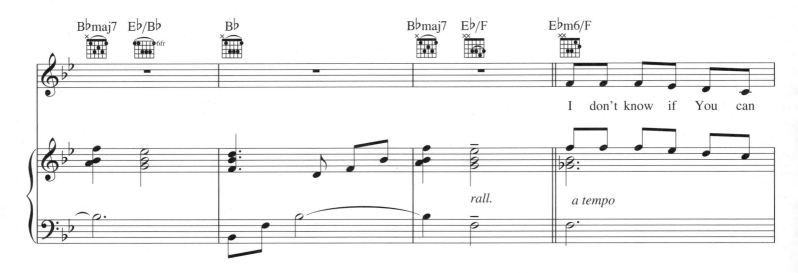

I don't know if You can

hear me or if You're e- ven there. I don't know if You will

lis - ten to a hum - ble prayer. They tell me I am just an

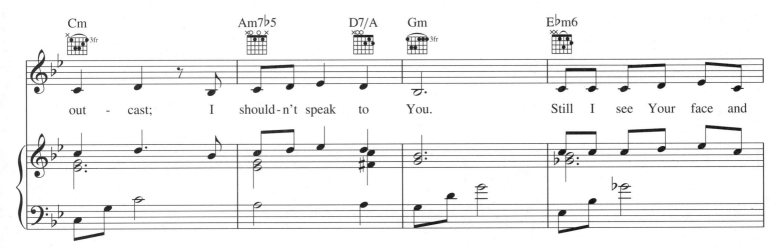

out - cast; I should-n't speak to You. Still I see Your face and

won - der: were You once an out - cast, too? _____

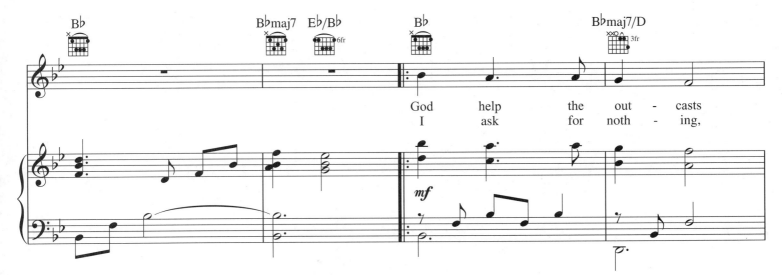

God help the out - casts
I ask for noth - ing,

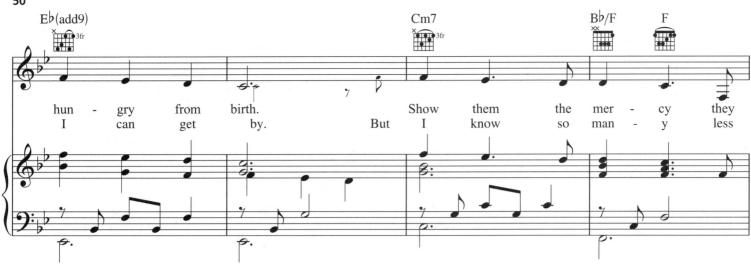

I can get by.
hun - gry from birth. But I them know so man - y they less
Show them the mer - cy they

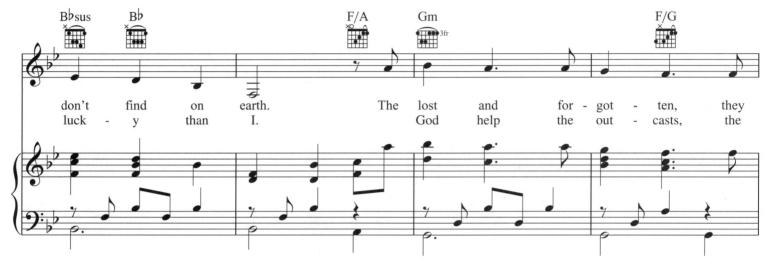

don't find on earth. The lost and for - got - ten, they
luck - y than I. God help the out - casts, the

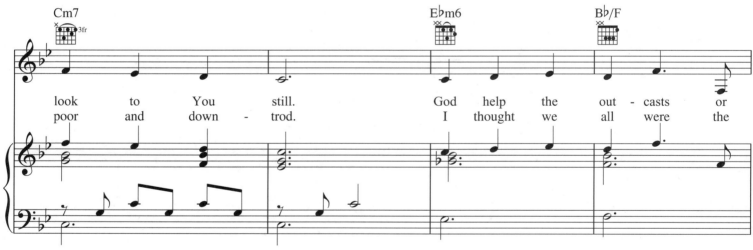

look to You still. God help the out - casts or
poor and down - trod. I thought we all were the

no - bod - y will.
chil - dren of

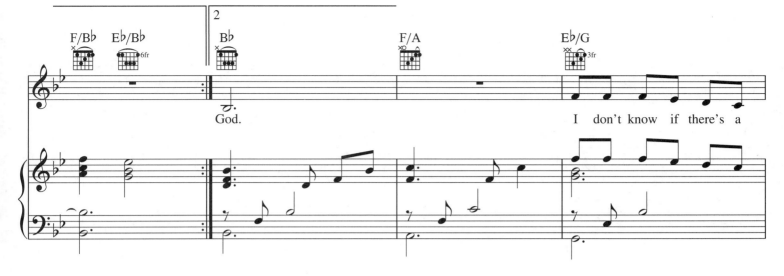

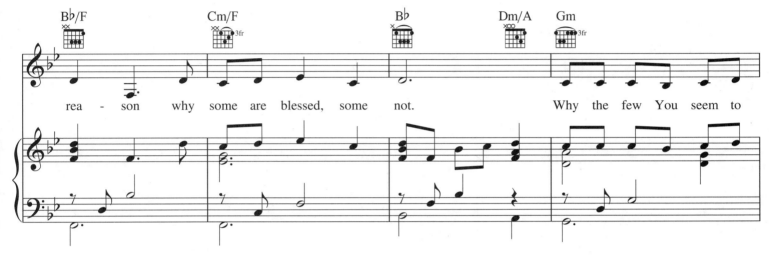

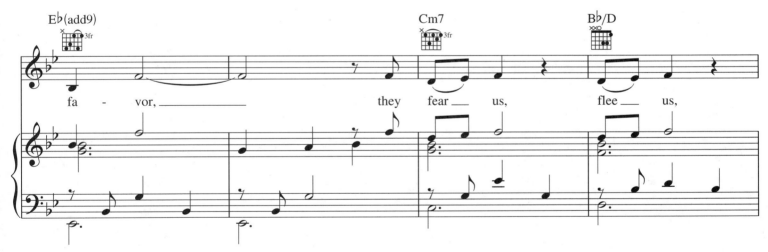

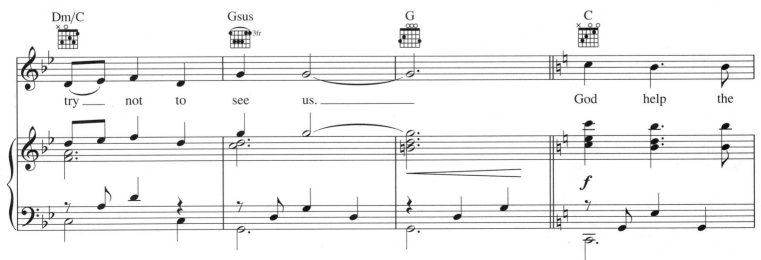

out - casts, the tat - tered, the torn, seek - ing an

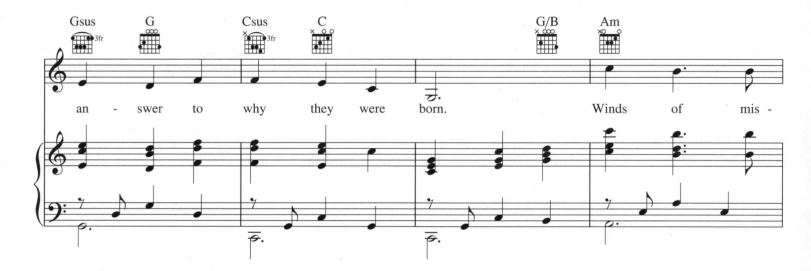

an - swer to why they were born. Winds of mis -

for - tune have blown them a - bout. You made the

dim.

out - casts; don't cast them out. The

poor and un-luck-y, the weak and the odd;____

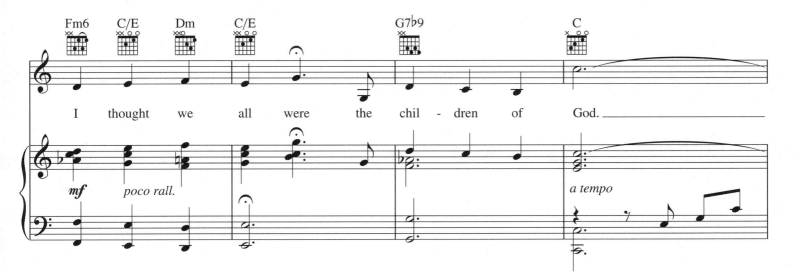

I thought we all were the chil-dren of God.____

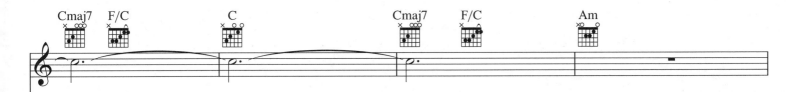

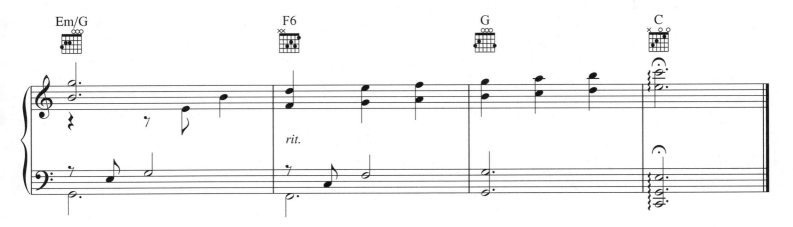

GOTTA GO MY OWN WAY

from the Disney Channel Original Movie HIGH SCHOOL MUSICAL 2

Words and Music by ADAM WATTS
and ANDY DODD

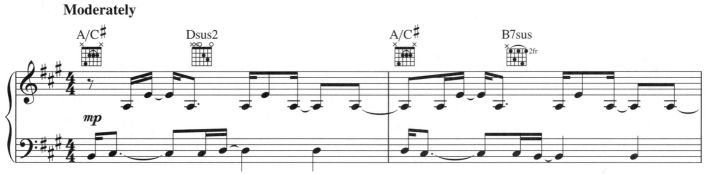

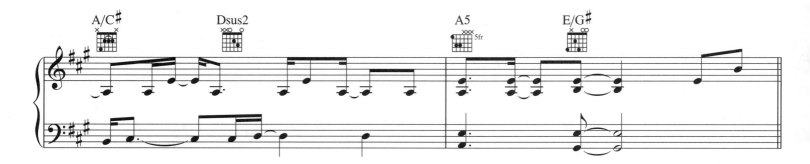

Gabriella: I got-ta say what's on __ my mind. __
Don't wan-na leave it all __ be - hind,

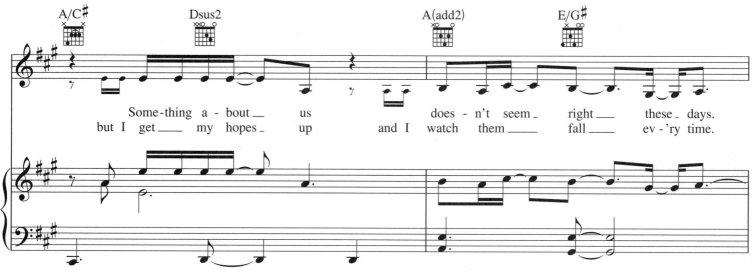

Some-thing a - bout __ us does - n't seem __ right __ these __ days.
but I get __ my hopes __ up and I watch them __ fall __ ev -'ry time.

I got-ta go my own ____ way. ____

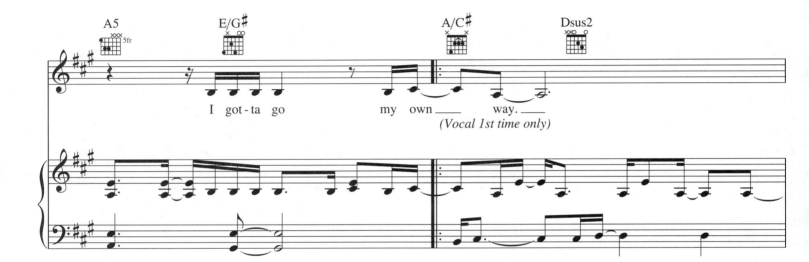

I got-ta go my own ____ way. ____
(Vocal 1st time only)

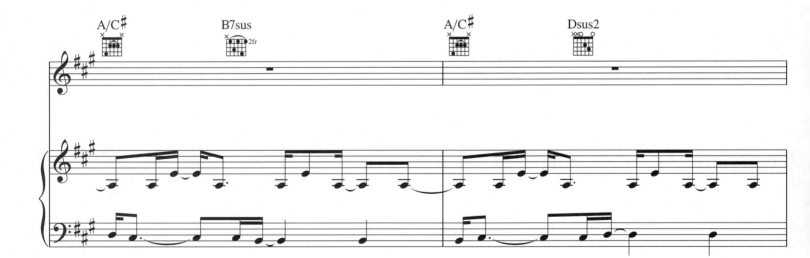

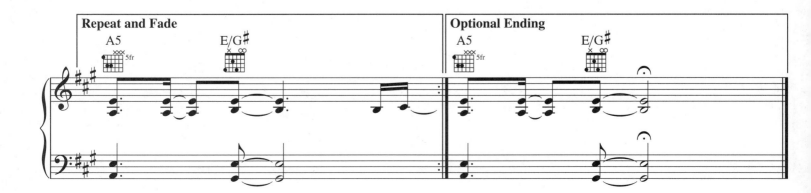

Repeat and Fade

Optional Ending

HOME

from Walt Disney's BEAUTY AND THE BEAST: THE BROADWAY MUSICAL

Music by ALAN MENKEN
Lyrics by TIM RICE

HAKUNA MATATA

from Walt Disney Pictures' THE LION KING

Music by ELTON JOHN
Lyrics by TIM RICE

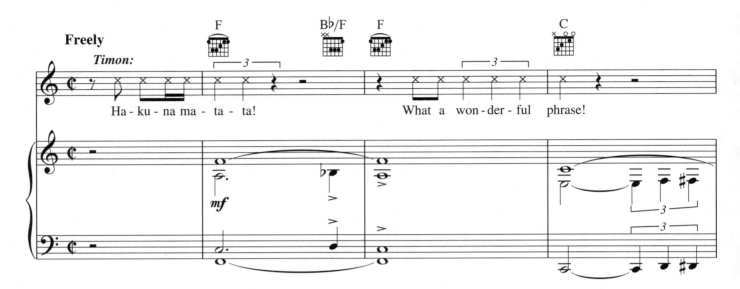

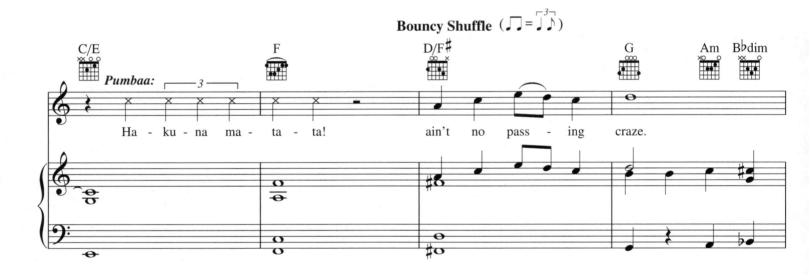

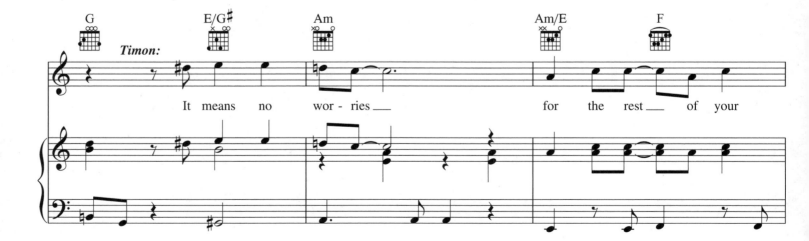

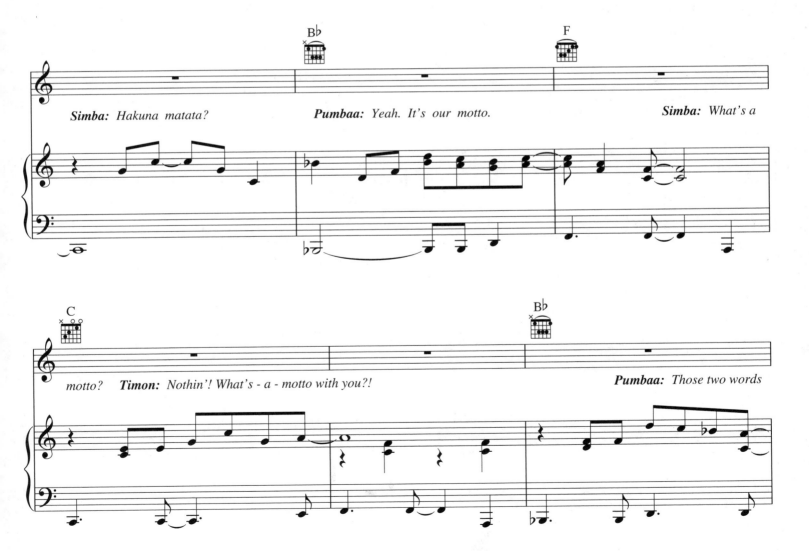

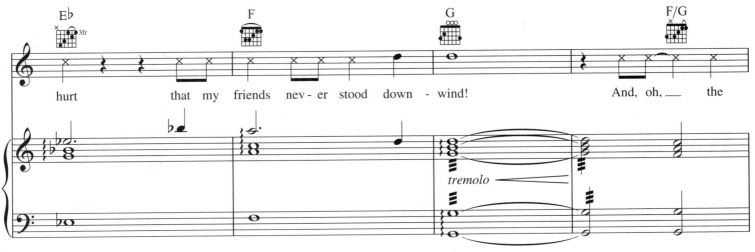

hurt ___ that my friends nev-er stood down-wind! And, oh, ___ the

shame! He was a - shamed! Thought of chang-in' my name. Oh, what's in a

name? And I got down - heart-ed. How did ya feel? ___ Ev - 'ry time that I...

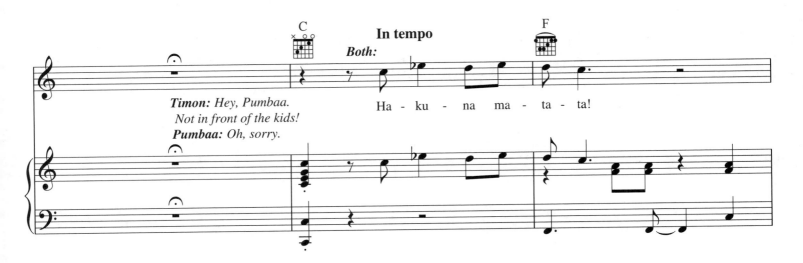

Timon: Hey, Pumbaa.
Not in front of the kids!
Pumbaa: Oh, sorry.

Ha - ku - na ma - ta - ta!

What a won-der-ful phrase. Ha-ku-na ma-ta-ta!

Young Simba:

ain't no pass-ing craze. It means no wor-ries

Young Simba, Timon & Pumbaa:

for the rest of your days. It's our prob-lem-free

Timon & Young Simba:

phi-los-o-phy. Ha-ku-na ma-ta-ta.

ku - na ma - ta - ta. Ha - ku - na ma - ta - ta. Ha - ku - na ma - ta - ta. Ha -

ku - na ma - ta - ta. Ha - ku - na ma - ta - ta.

Young Simba:

It means no

wor - ries _____ for the rest _ of your days. _

All:

It's our

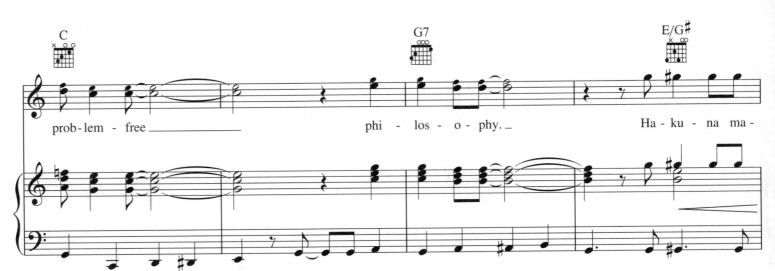

prob - lem - free _____ phi - los - o - phy. _ Ha - ku - na ma -

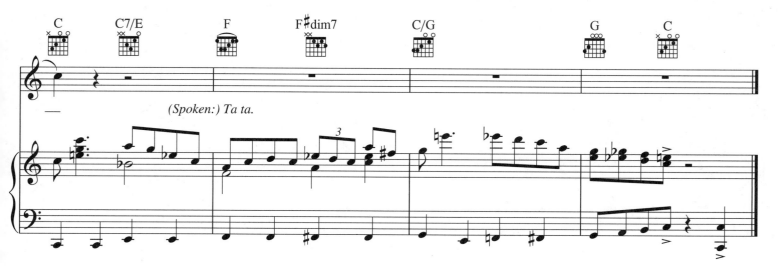

HAWAIIAN ROLLER COASTER RIDE

from Walt Disney's LILO & STITCH

Words and Music by ALAN SILVESTRI
and MARK KEALI'I HO'OMALU

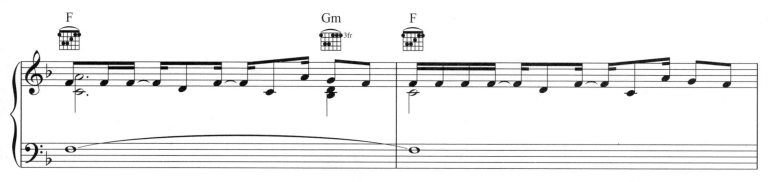

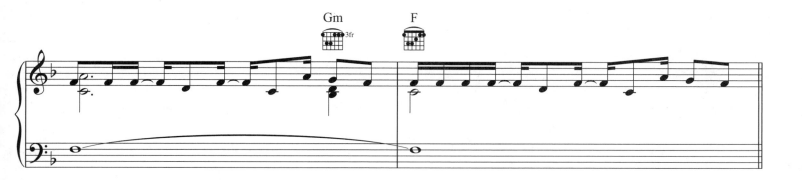

1.,3. *Lead:* There's no___ place I'd rath - er be ___ *Chorus:* than on my surf - board out at sea.
2. *All:* There's no ___ place I'd rath - er be ___ *Chorus:* than on the sea - shore dry, wet, free.

*Children's Chorus

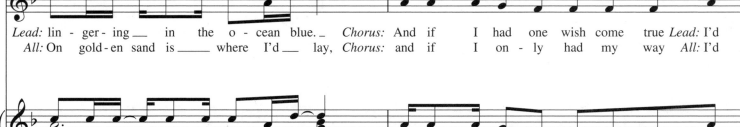

Lead: lin - ger - ing ___ in the o - cean blue. ___ *Chorus:* And if I had one wish come true *Lead:* I'd
All: On gold - en sand is ___ where I'd ___ lay, *Chorus:* and if I on - ly had my way *All:* I'd

Chorus: La - we mai i ko pa - pa he - 'e na - lu. Pi' - i na lu - lu la la - ha - la - ha. O __
No wor - ry, no __ fear. Ain't __ no big - gy, brah - da. Put - tin' in, cut - tin' up, cut - tin' back, cut - tin' out.

Lead: __ ka mo - a - na ha - nu - pa - nu - pa. La - la - la i ka la ha - na - ha - na. Me __
Front side, back side, __ goof - y - foot - ed wipe out.

Chorus:

Lead: __ ke kai ho - en - e __ i ka pu - 'e one. *Lead:* He - le - he - le mai ka - kou e.

Chorus: Ha - wai - ian roll - er coast - er ride. Let's go jump - in', surf's __ up and pump - in'.

Coast - in' with the mo - tion of the o - cean. Whirl - pools swirl - ing, cas - cad - ing, swirl - ing.

Chorus: Ha - wai - ian roll - er coast - er ride. *Slide guitar ad lib.*

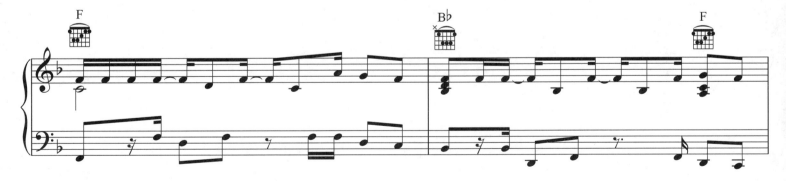

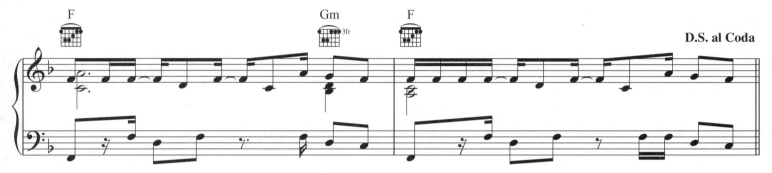

D.S. al Coda

CODA

Lead: La - la - la i ka la ha - na - ha - na. *Chorus:* Me __ ke kai ho - en - e __ i ka pu – 'e one.

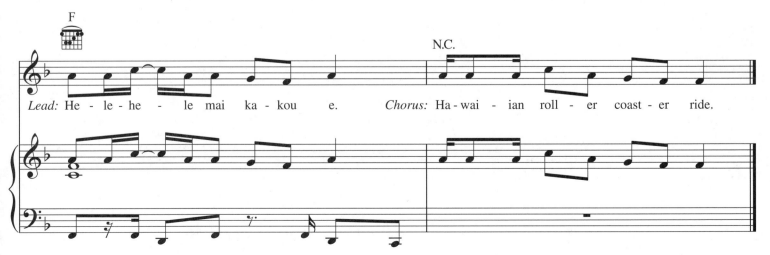

N.C.

Lead: He - le - he — le mai ka - kou e. *Chorus:* Ha - wai – ian roll - er coast - er ride.

IF I CAN'T LOVE HER

from Walt Disney's BEAUTY AND THE BEAST: THE BROADWAY MUSICAL

Music by ALAN MENKEN
Lyrics by TIM RICE

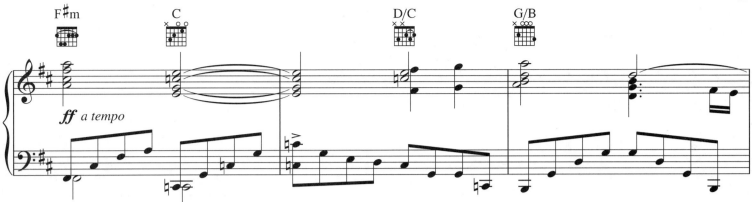

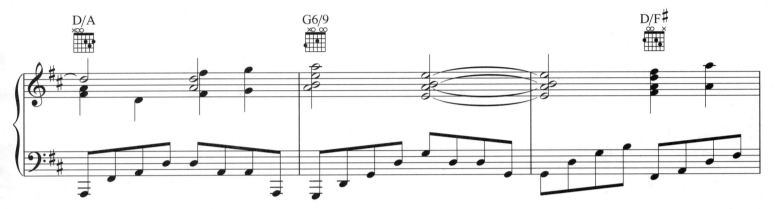

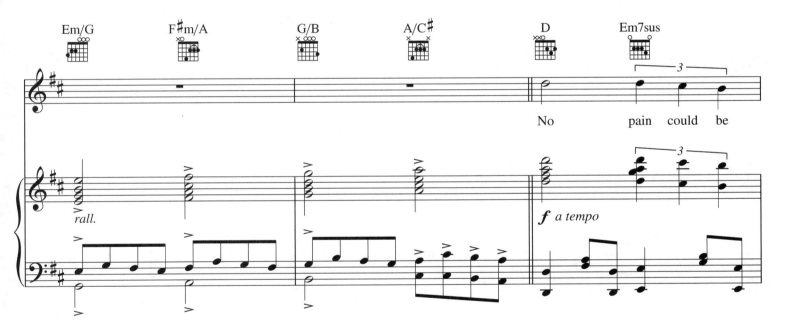

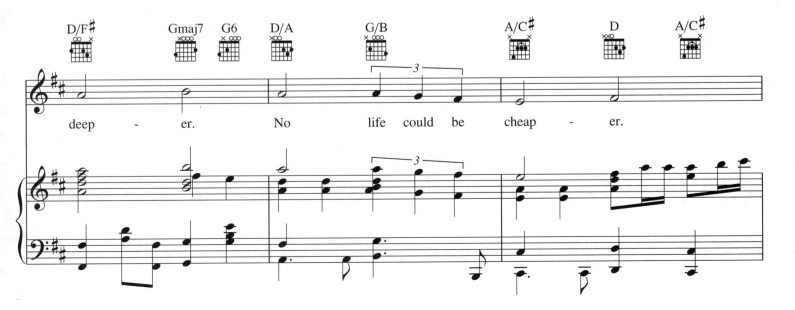

IF I DIDN'T HAVE YOU

Walt Disney Pictures Presents A Pixar Animation Studios Film MONSTERS, INC.

Music and Lyrics by
RANDY NEWMAN

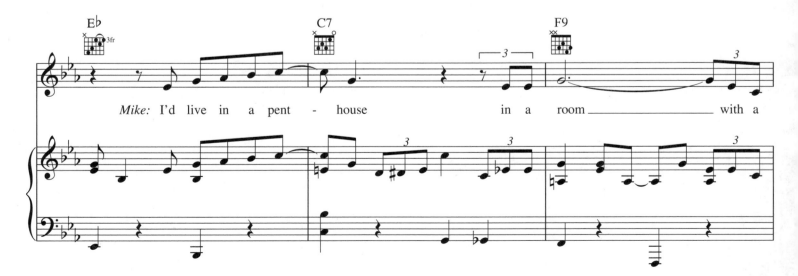

IF I NEVER KNEW YOU
(Love Theme from POCAHONTAS)
from Walt Disney's POCAHONTAS

Music by ALAN MENKEN
Lyrics by STEPHEN SCHWARTZ

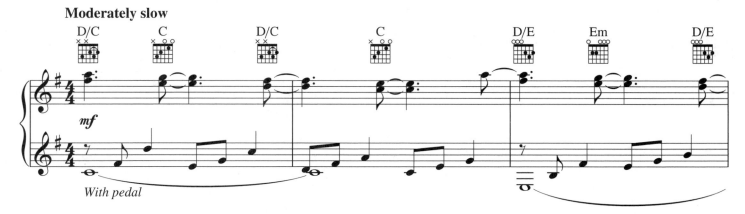

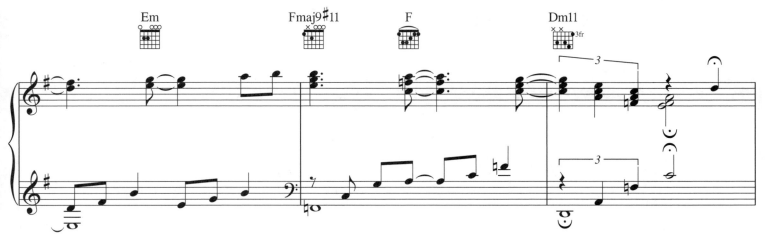

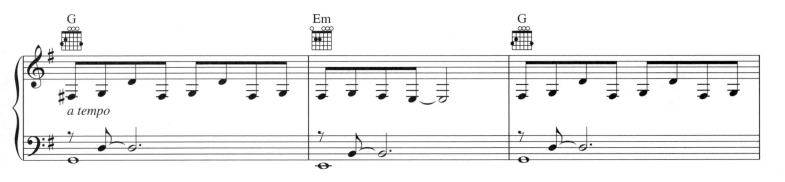

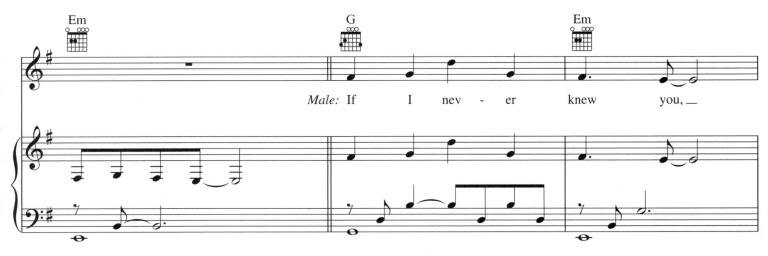

Male: If I nev-er knew you, —

if I nev - er felt ____ this love, ____ I would have no ink-

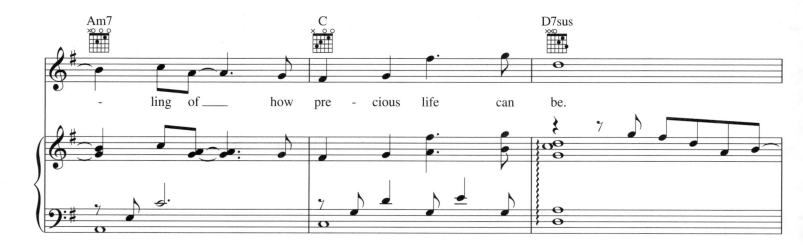

- ling of ____ how pre - cious life can be.

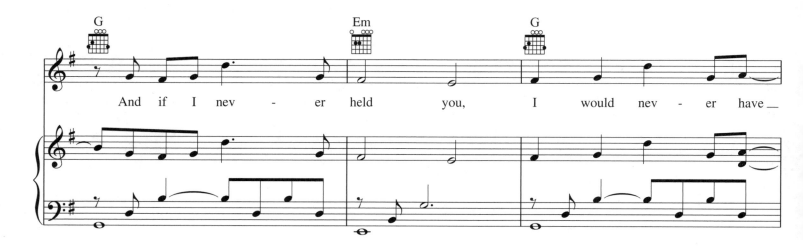

And if I nev - er held you, I would nev - er have ____

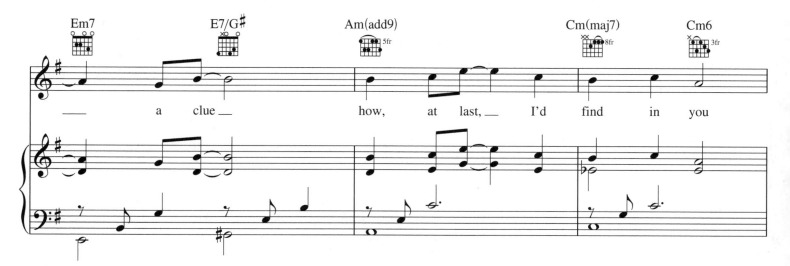

____ a clue ____ how, at last, ____ I'd find in you

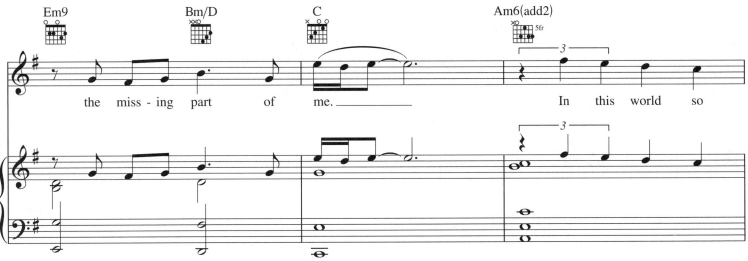

the miss-ing part of me. _____ In this world so

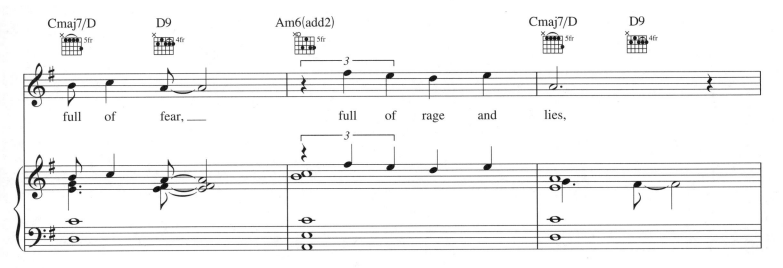

full of fear, ___ full of rage and lies,

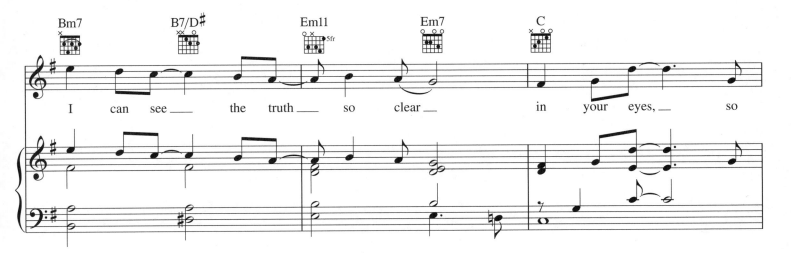

I can see ___ the truth ___ so clear ___ in your eyes, ___ so

dry your eyes. ___ And I'm so grate-ful to you.

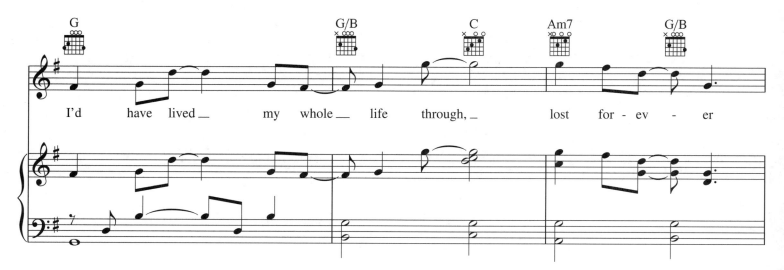

I'd have lived __ my whole __ life through, __ lost for - ev - er

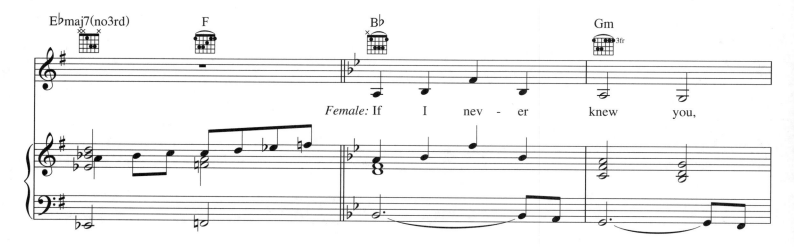

if I nev - er knew __ you. _____

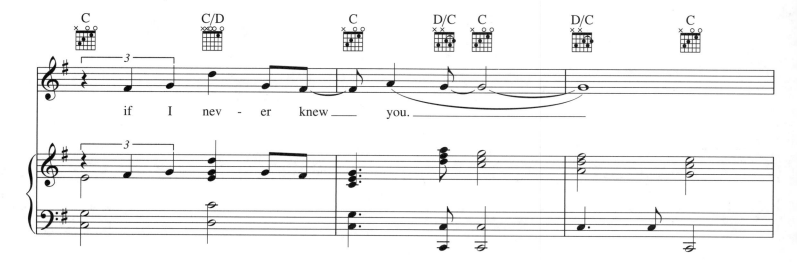

Female: If I nev - er knew you,

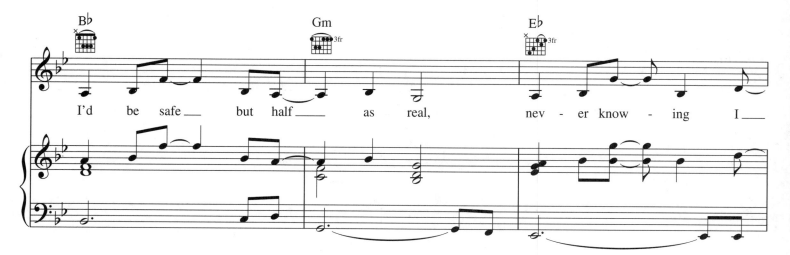

I'd be safe __ but half __ as real, nev - er know - ing I __

could feel ___ a love so strong ___ and true.

I'm so grate - ful to you. I'd have lived ___ my whole ___

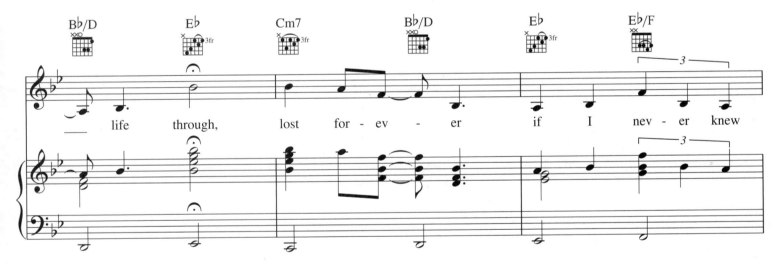

life through, lost for - ev - er if I nev - er knew

Male: I ___ thought our love would be so beau - ti - ful.
you. ___

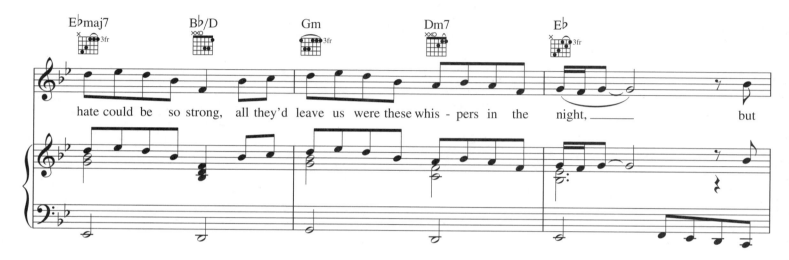

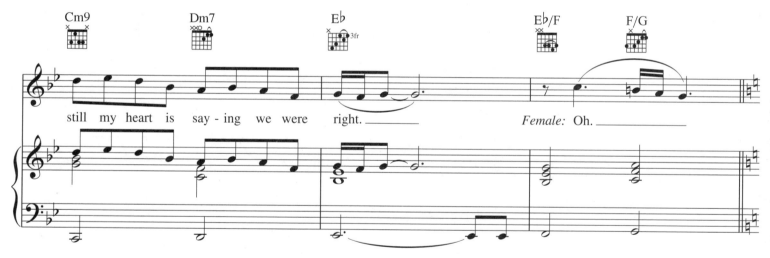

since the mo - ment that we met. __ If our time has
___ this love, __ I would have __ no ink - ling of ___ how

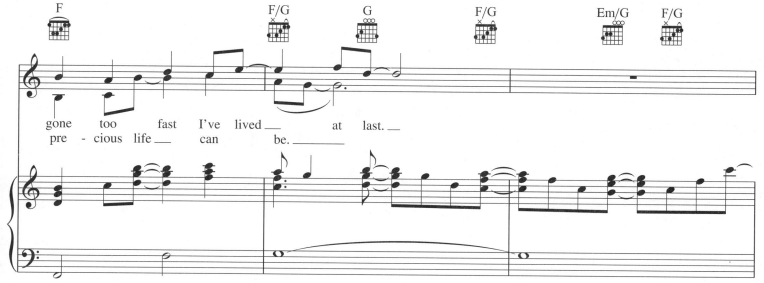

gone too fast I've lived __ at last. __
pre - cious life __ can be. ___

Both: I thought our love would be so

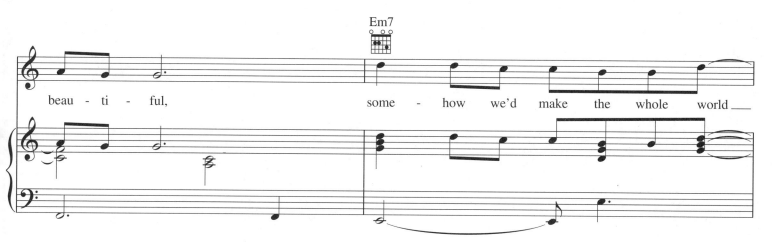

beau - ti - ful, some - how we'd make the whole world ___

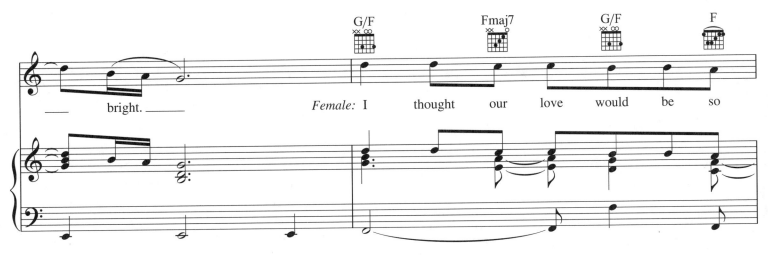

bright. _____ *Female:* I thought our love would be so

beau - ti - ful, we'd turn the dark - ness in - to _____ light. _____ *Both:* And

still my heart is say - ing we were right. _____ *Male:* We were right. And

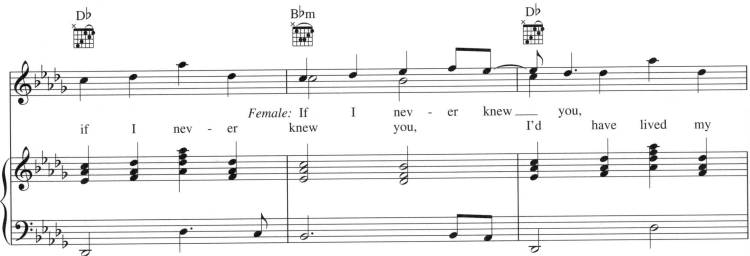

Female: If I nev - er knew _____ you,

if I nev - er knew you, I'd have lived my

IF WE WERE A MOVIE

Words and Music by JEANNIE LURIE
and HOLLY MATHIS

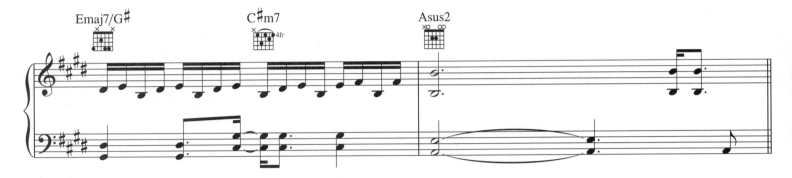

Uh - oh, ___ there you go a - gain, ___ talk - in' cin - e - mat - ic.
Yeah, yeah, ___ when you call me ___ I can hear it in ___ your

Yeah, you, ___ you're charm - ing, got ev' - ry - bod - y star - struck.
voice. Oh, sure, ___ want to see me ___ and tell me all a - bout her.

we'd be laugh - ing, watch - ing the sun - set fade to black,

show the names, play the hap - py song.

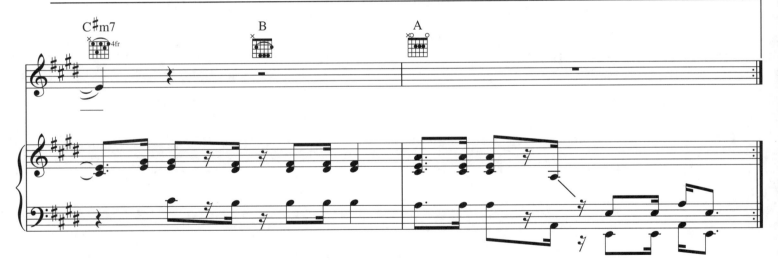

hap - py song. Wish I could tell you there's a twist,

some kind of he - ro in dis - guise, __ and we're to - geth - er, it's for

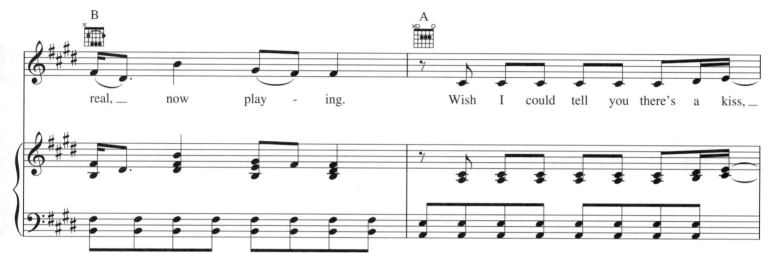

real, __ now play - ing. Wish I could tell you there's a kiss, __

__ like some - thing more __ than in __ my mind. __ I see __ it

could be a - maz - ing. (Could be a - maz - ing if we were a mov - If

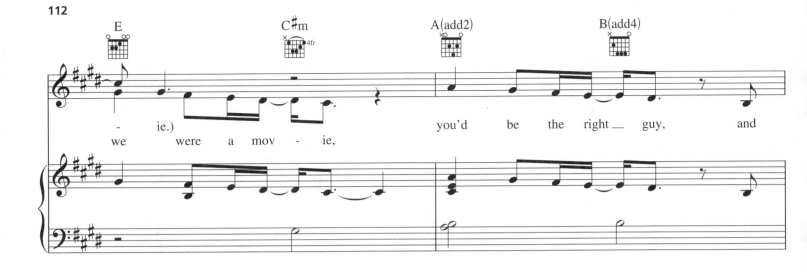

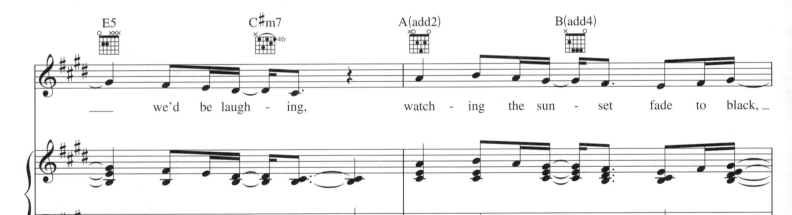

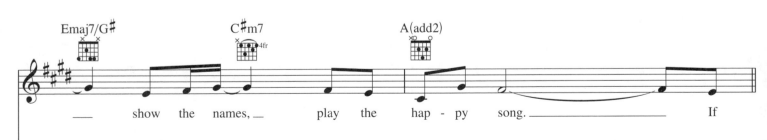

LES POISSONS

from Walt Disney's THE LITTLE MERMAID

Music by ALAN MENKEN
Lyrics by HOWARD ASHMAN

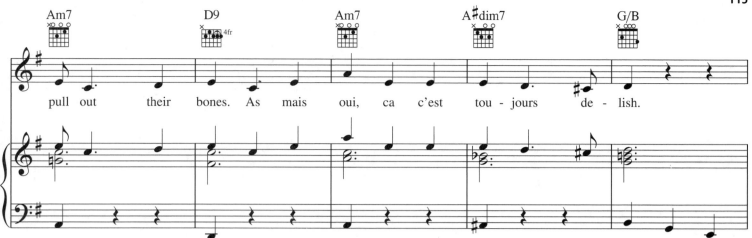

pull out their bones. As mais oui, ca c'est tou - jours de - lish.

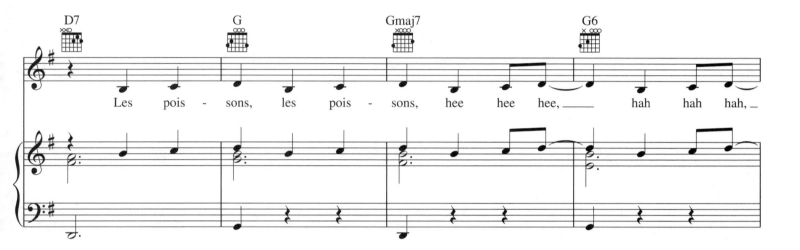

Les pois - sons, les pois - sons, hee hee hee, _____ hah hah hah, _

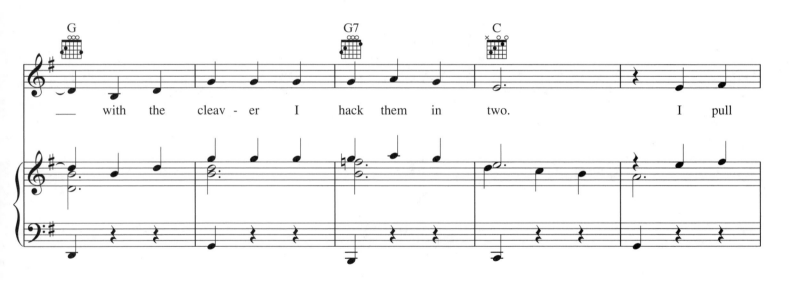

_ with the cleav - er I hack them in two. I pull

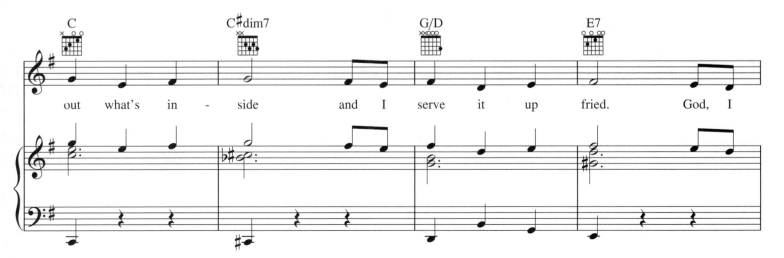

out what's in - side and I serve it up fried. God, I

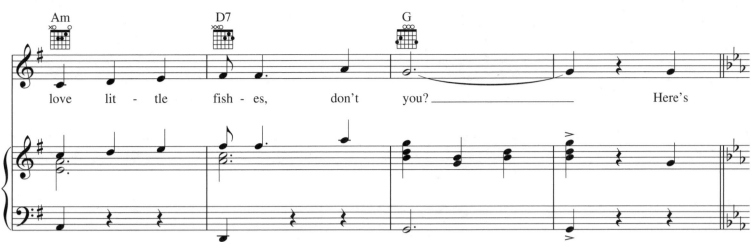

love lit - tle fish - es, don't you? _____ Here's

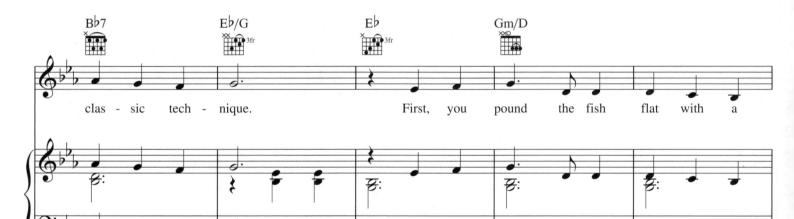

some - thing for tempt - ing the pal - ate, _____ pre - pared in the

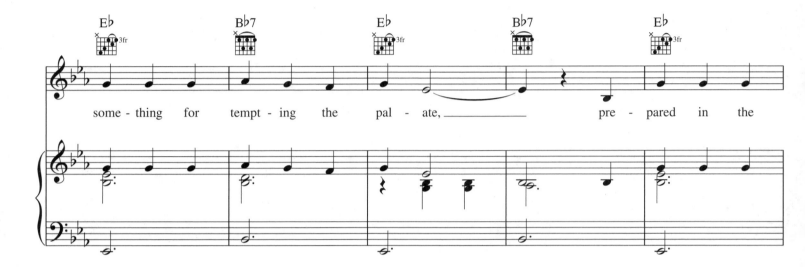

clas - sic tech - nique. First, you pound the fish flat with a

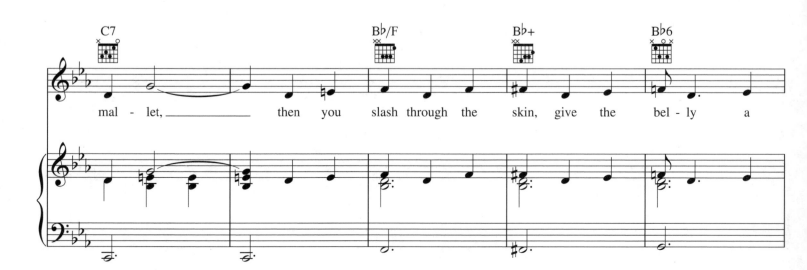

mal - let, _____ then you slash through the skin, give the bel - ly a

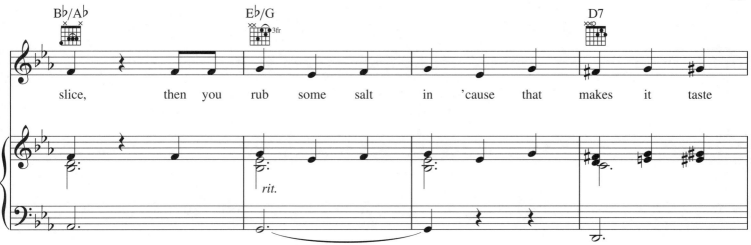

slice, then you rub some salt in 'cause that makes it taste

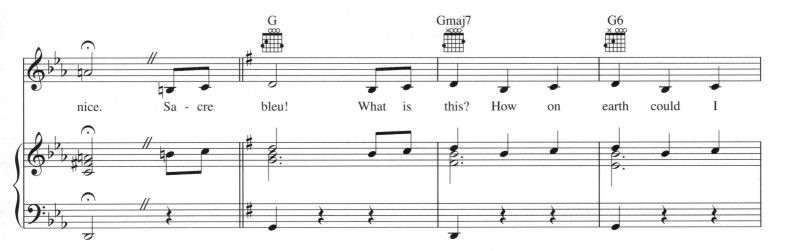

nice. Sa - cre bleu! What is this? How on earth could I

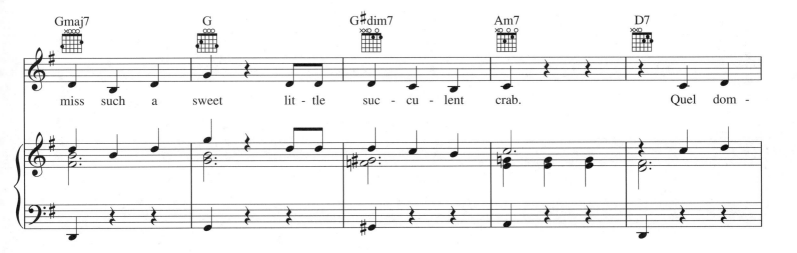

miss such a sweet lit - tle suc - cu - lent crab. Quel dom -

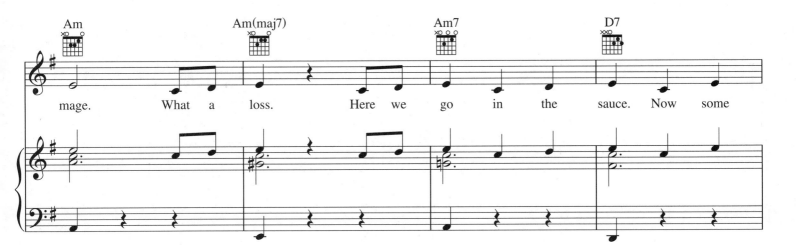

mage. What a loss. Here we go in the sauce. Now some

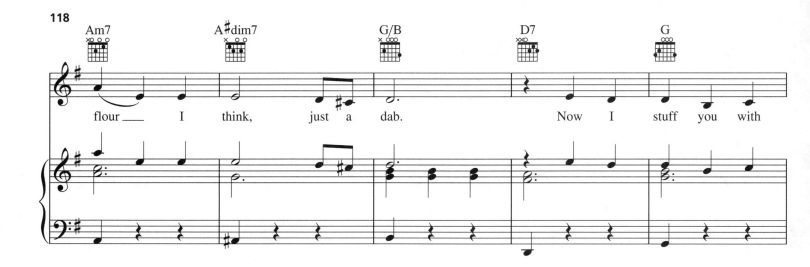

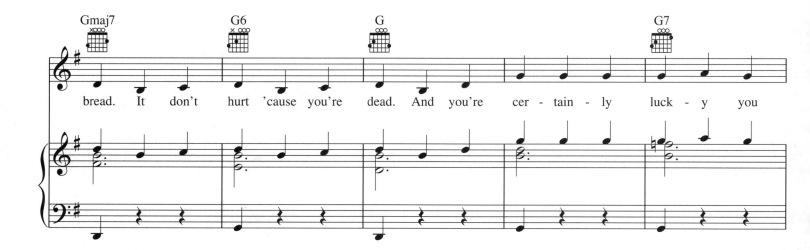

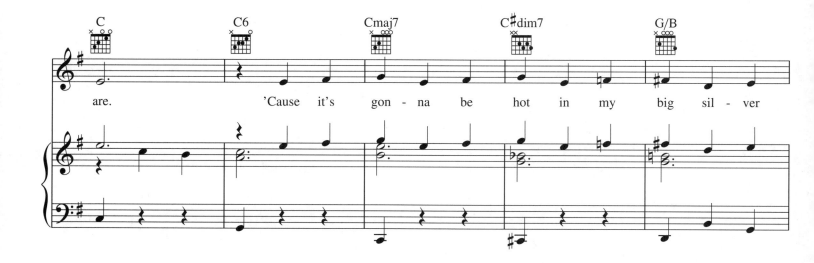

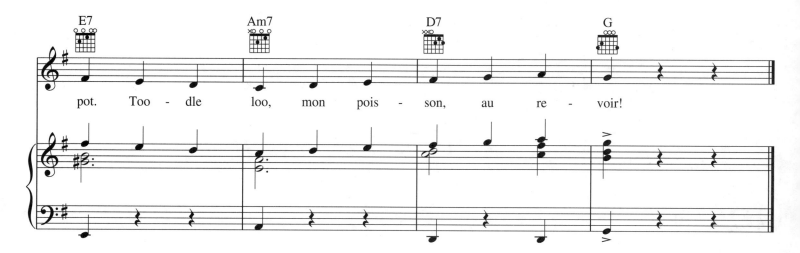

THE INCREDITS

from Walt Disney Pictures' THE INCREDIBLES – A Pixar Film

Music by MICHAEL GIACCHINO

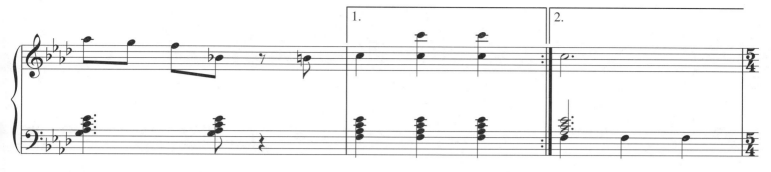

Sax solo ad lib.

Sax solo ends

gliss.

JUST AROUND THE RIVERBEND

from Walt Disney's POCAHONTAS

Music by ALAN MENKEN
Lyrics by STEPHEN SCHWARTZ

With motion

Lyrics:

What I love most a-bout riv-ers is: ___ you can't step in the same riv-er twice. ___ The wa-ter's al-ways chang-ing, al-ways flow-ing. ___ But peo-ple, I guess, can't live like that; ___ we

all must pay a price: _ to be safe we lose our chance of ev - er

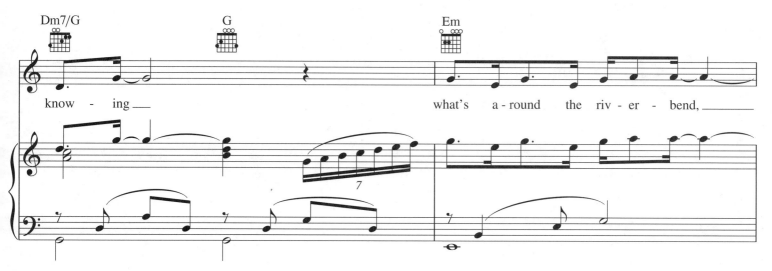

know - ing ___ what's a - round the riv - er - bend, _____

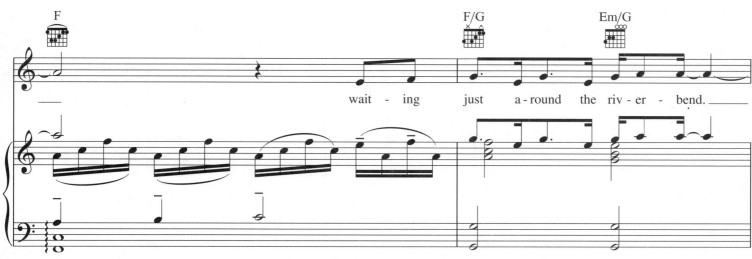

___ wait - ing just a - round the riv - er - bend. _____

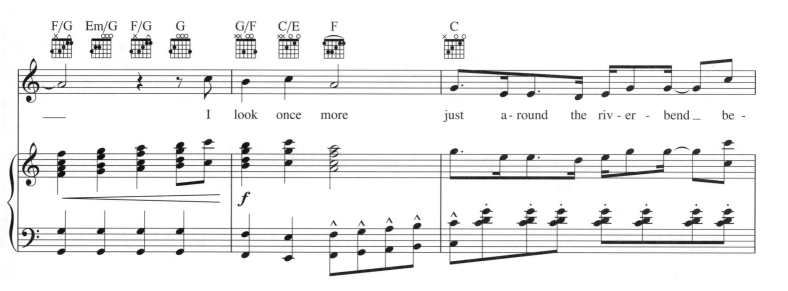

___ I look once more just a - round the riv - er - bend _ be -

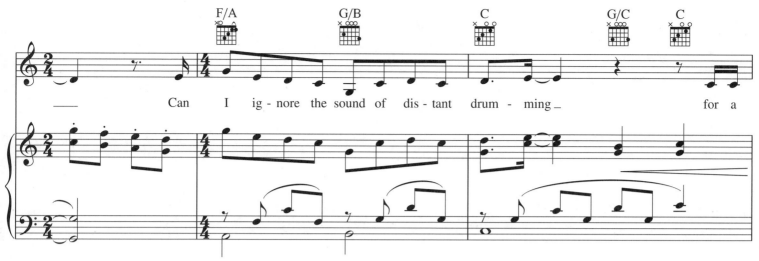

Can I ig - nore the sound of dis - tant drum - ming _ for a

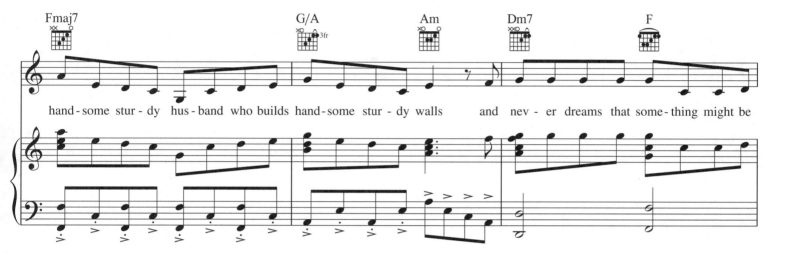

hand - some stur - dy hus - band who builds hand - some stur - dy walls and nev - er dreams that some - thing might be

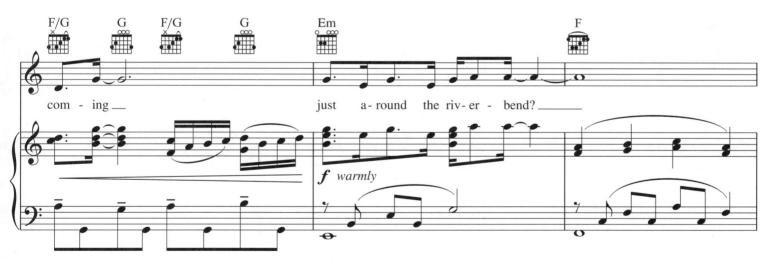

com - ing _ just a - round the riv - er - bend? _

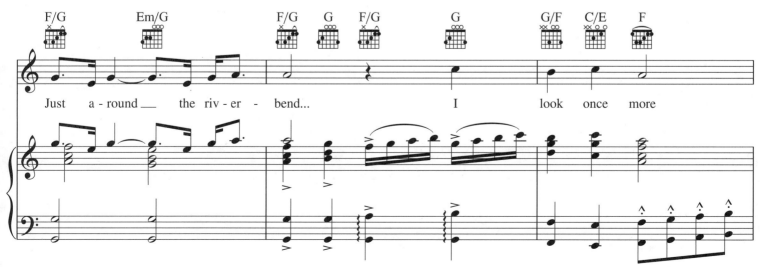

Just a - round _ the riv - er - bend... I look once more

Should I mar-ry Ko-co-um? _____ Is all my dream-ing at an end? _____ Or

Più mosso

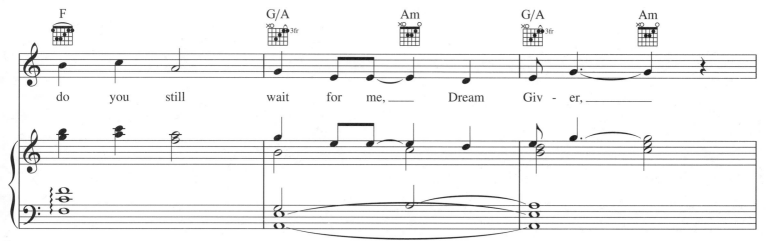

do you still wait for me, _____ Dream Giv-er, _____

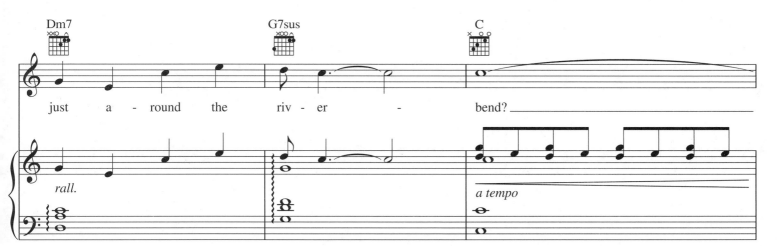

just a-round the riv-er - bend? _____

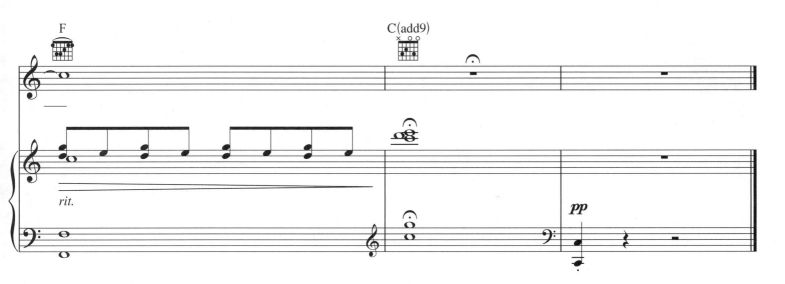

LOOK THROUGH MY EYES

from Walt Disney Pictures' BROTHER BEAR

Words and Music by
PHIL COLLINS

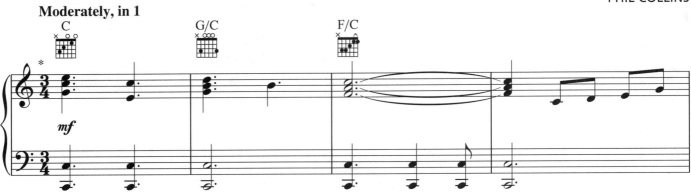

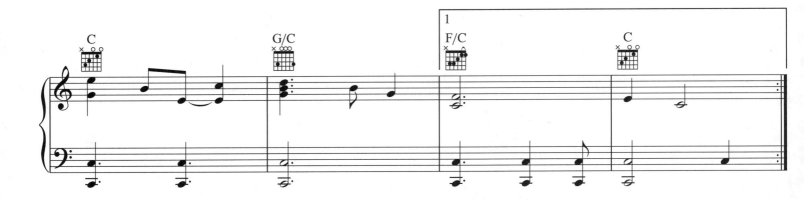

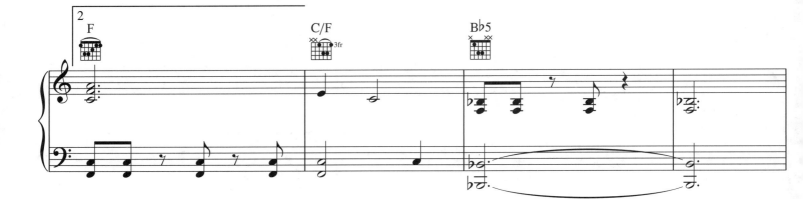

There   are   things   in

*Recorded a whole step higher.

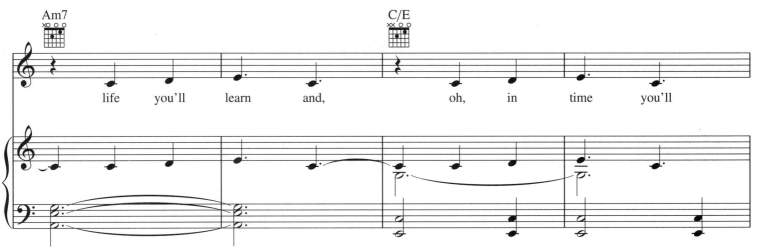

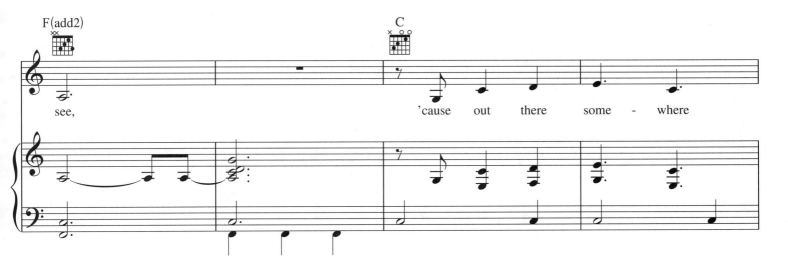

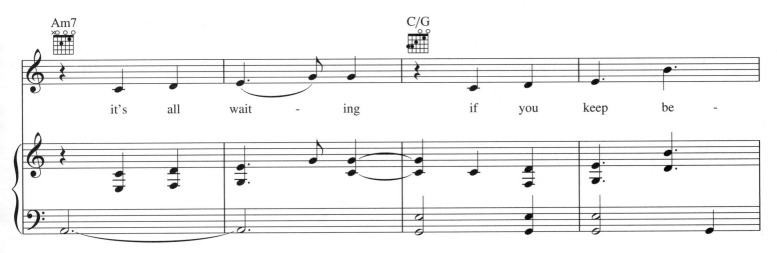

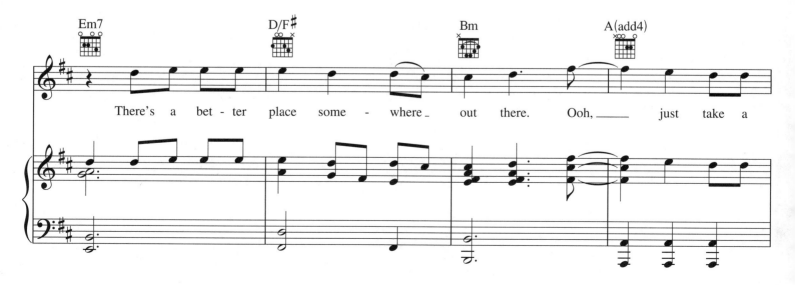

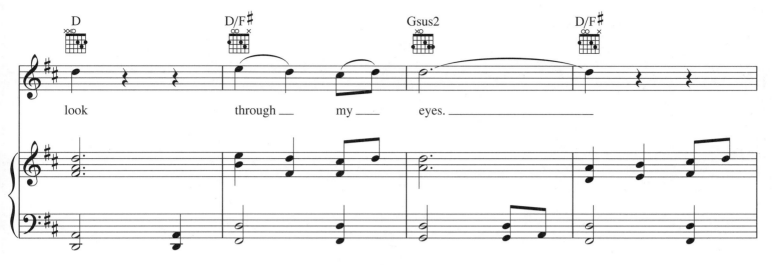

look through ___ my ___ eyes. _____

Ev - 'ry - thing chang - es. You'll be a - mazed what you'll

find _____ if you look through my ___

eyes. _____

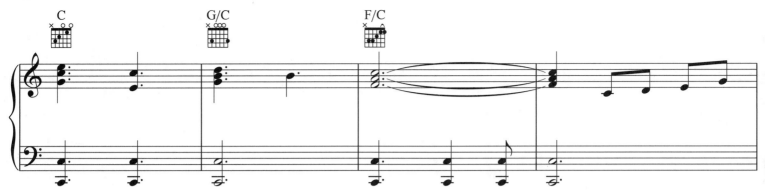

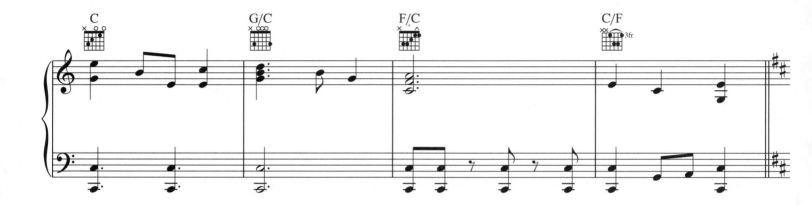

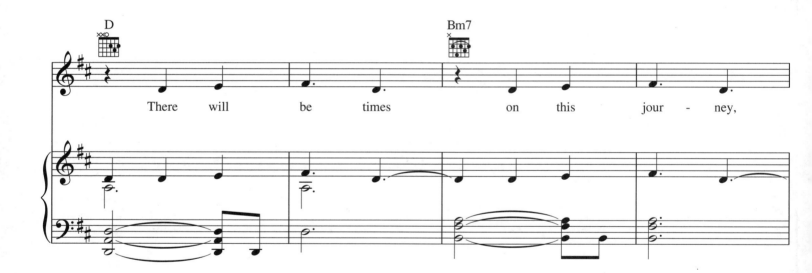

There will be times on this jour - ney,

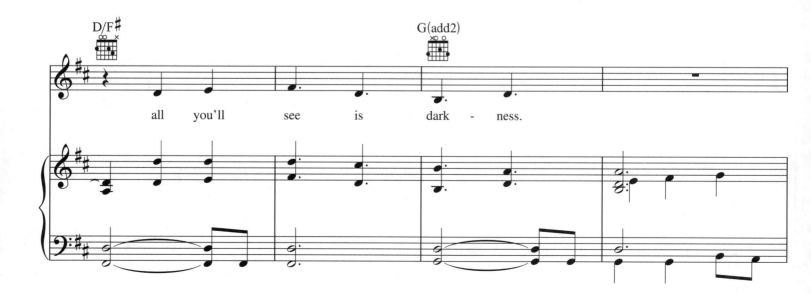

all you'll see is dark - ness.

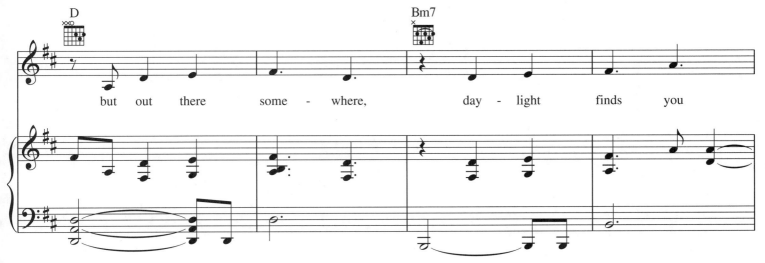

but out there some - where, day - light finds you

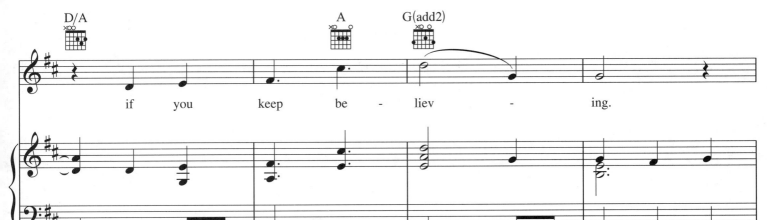

if you keep be - liev - ing.

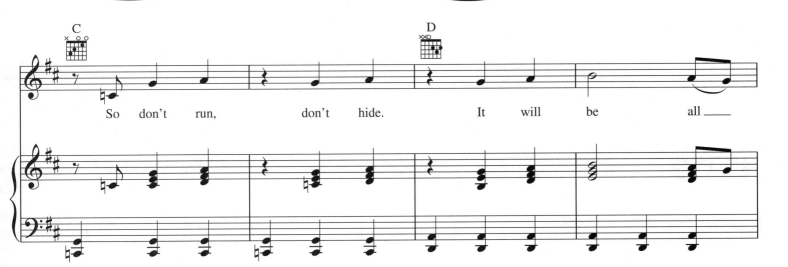

So don't run, don't hide. It will be all ____

right. You'll see; trust me. I'll be there _____

mazed what you'll find   if you look through my __

eyes. __

All the things that   you can change,   there's a

mean - ing in ev - 'ry - thing,   and you

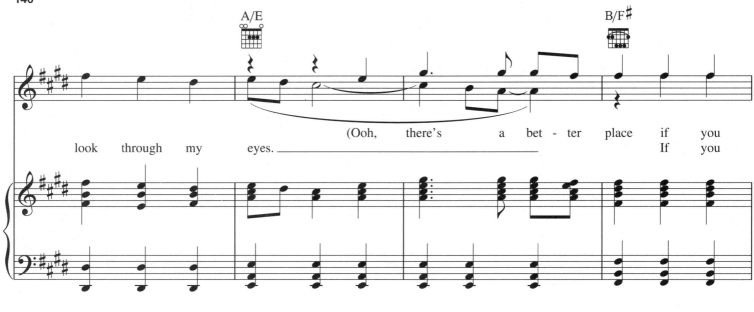

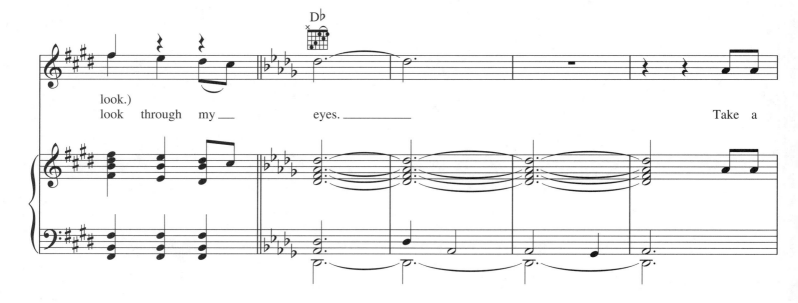

THE MEDALLION CALLS

from Walt Disney Pictures' PIRATES OF THE CARIBBEAN: THE CURSE OF THE BLACK PEARL

Music by KLAUS BADELT

Moderately

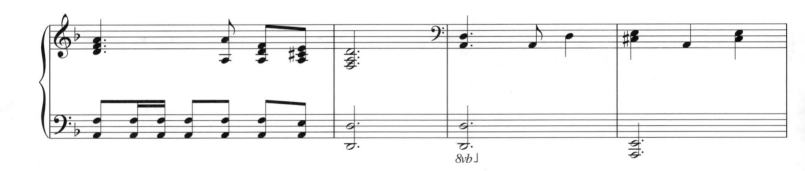

MY FUNNY FRIEND AND ME

from Walt Disney Pictures' THE EMPEROR'S NEW GROOVE

Lyrics by STING
Music by STING and DAVID HARTLEY

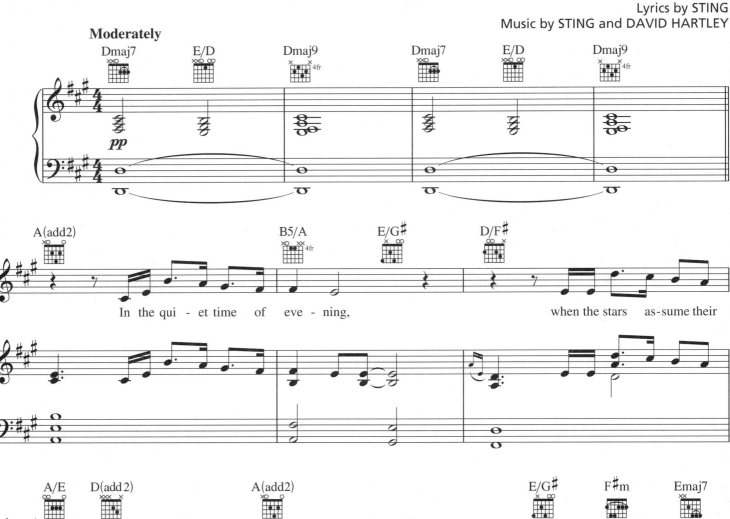

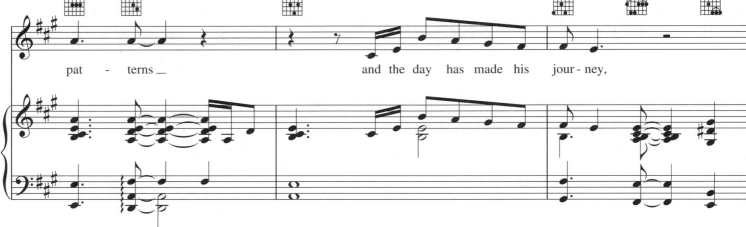

145

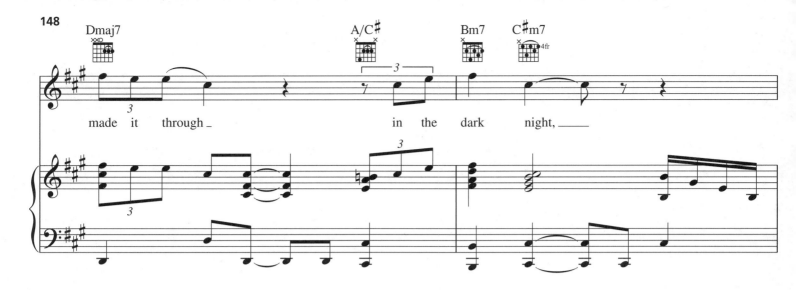

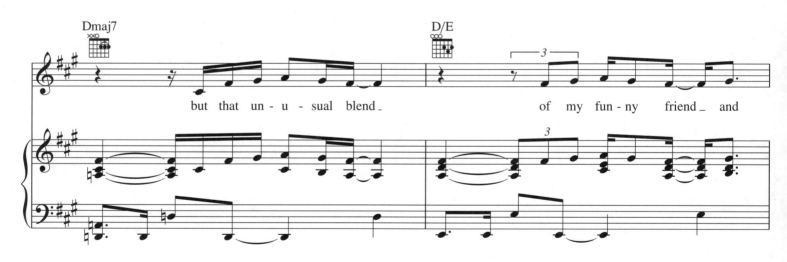

I'm not as clev-er as I thought I was.

I'm not the boy I used to be, be - cause

you showed me some-thing dif-f'rent; you showed me some-thing pure.

I al - ways seemed so cer-tain, but I was real - ly nev-er sure. But you

stayed, __ and you called my name _____

when oth-ers would have walked out on a lous - y game.

And look who made it through but your fun-ny friend __ and

you. You see the pat-terns in the big sky. _____

Those con-stel-la-tions look like you and I.

That ti-ny plan-et and the big-ger guy.

I don't know wheth-er I should laugh or cry.

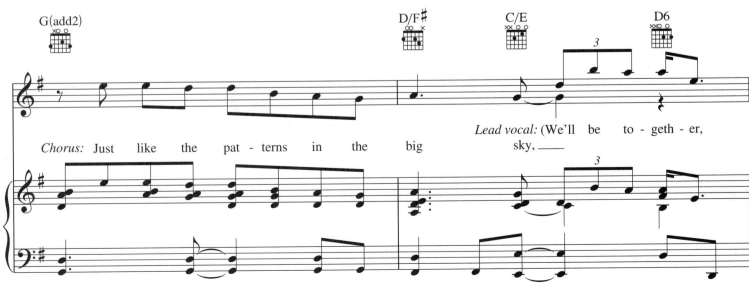

Chorus: Just like the pat-terns in the big

Lead vocal: (We'll be to-geth-er,

sky,

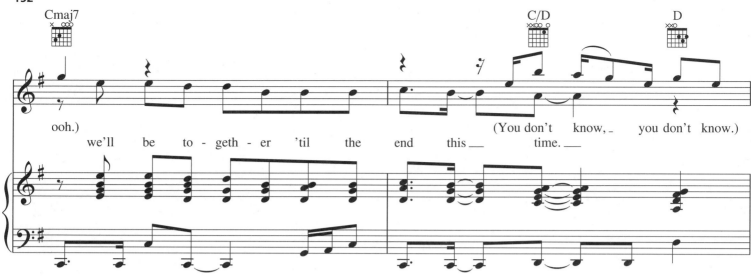

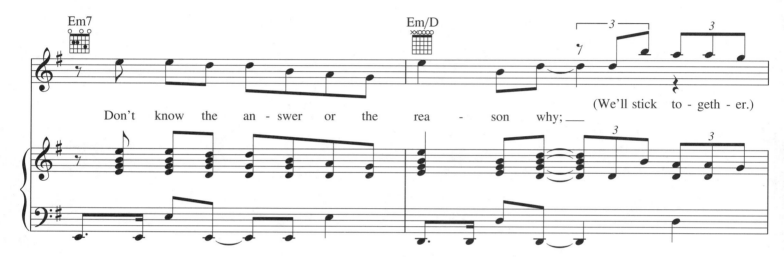

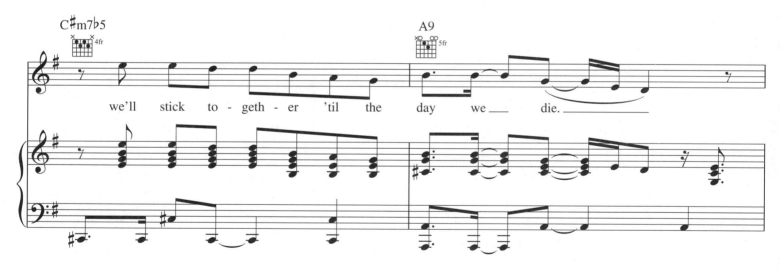

PART OF YOUR WORLD
from Walt Disney's THE LITTLE MERMAID

Music by ALAN MENKEN
Lyrics by HOWARD ASHMAN

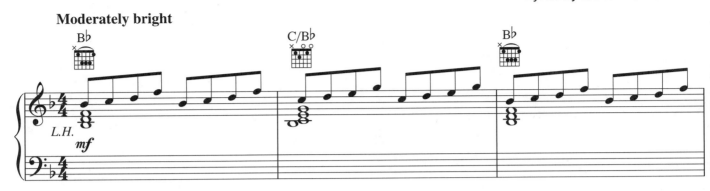

Look at this stuff. __ Is - n't it neat? __

Would-n't you think __ my col - lec - tion's com - plete?

Would-n't you think __ I'm the girl,

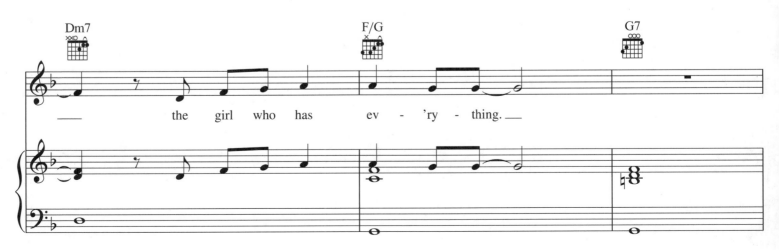

__ the girl who has ev - 'ry - thing. __

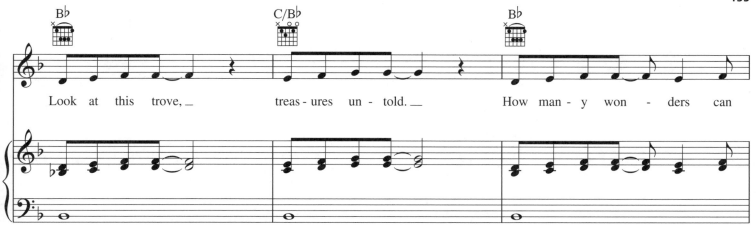

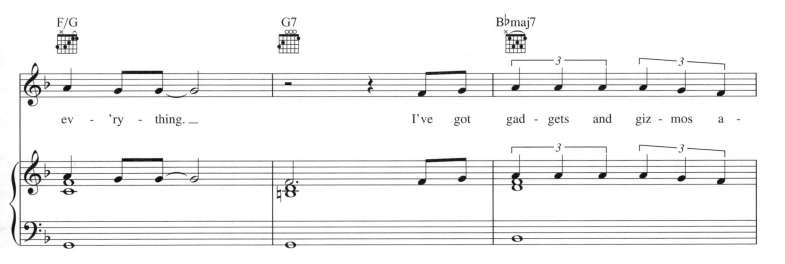

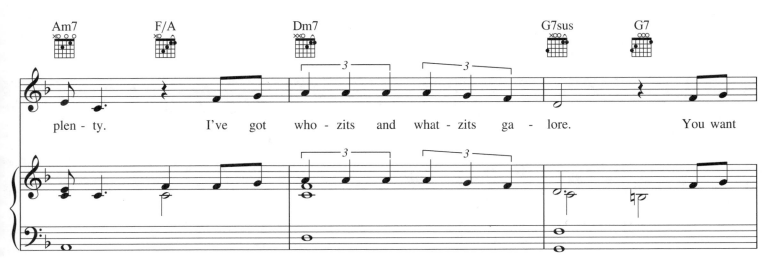

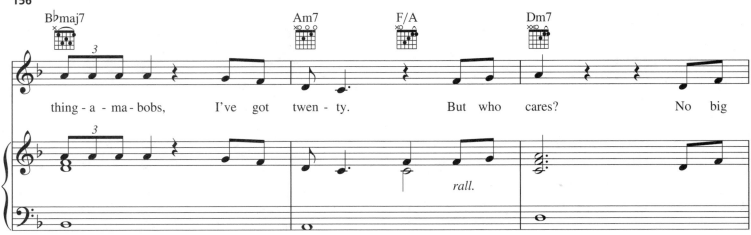

thing - a - ma - bobs, I've got twen - ty. But who cares? No big

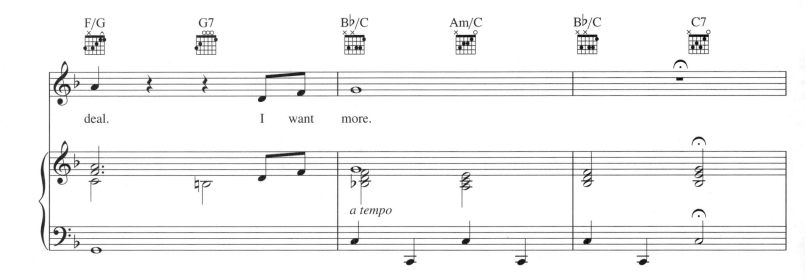

deal. I want more.

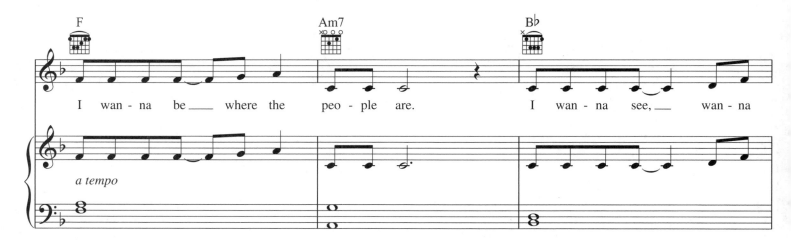

I wan - na be ___ where the peo - ple are. I wan - na see, ___ wan - na

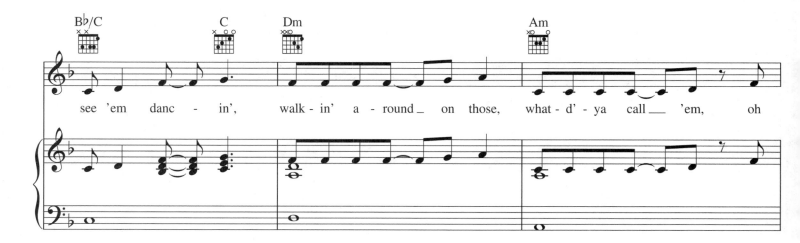

see 'em danc - in', walk - in' a - round ___ on those, what - d' - ya call ___ 'em, oh

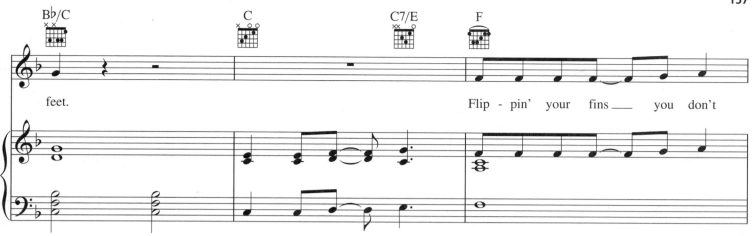

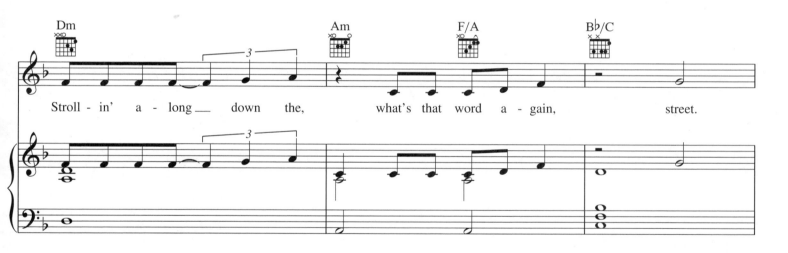

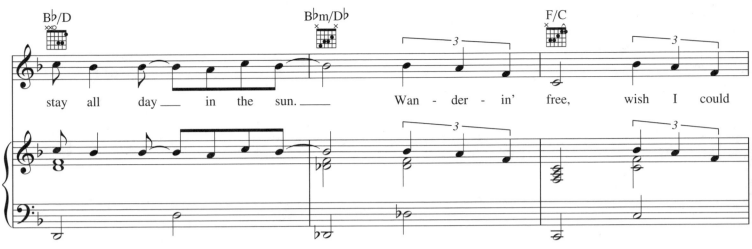

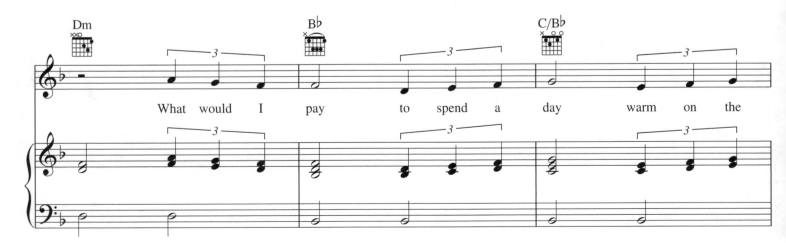

159

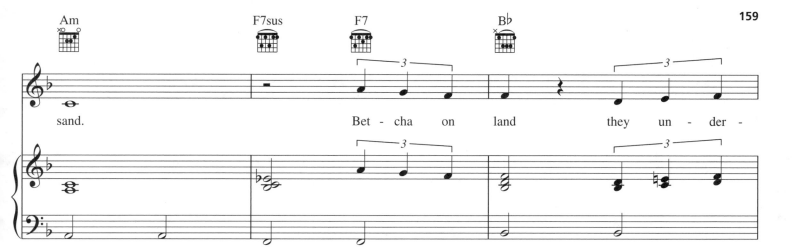

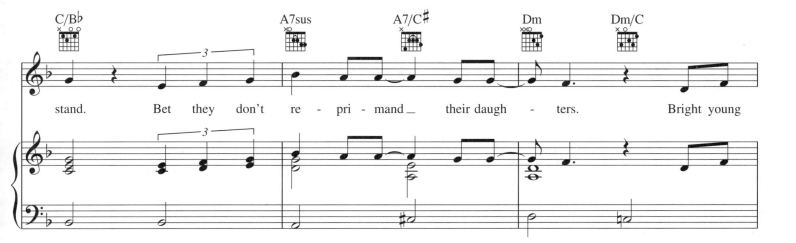

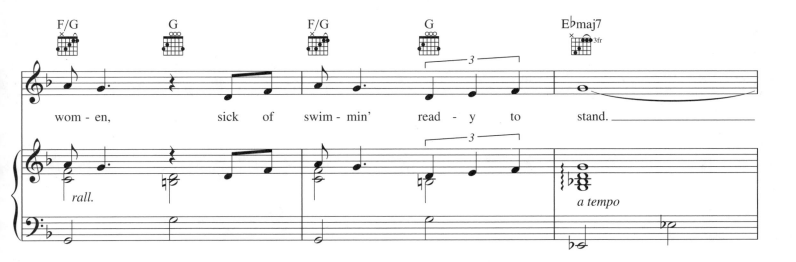

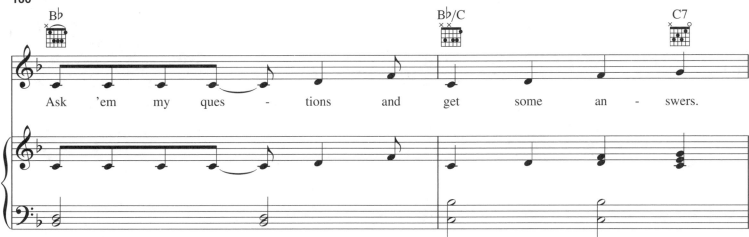

Ask 'em my ques - tions and get some an - swers.

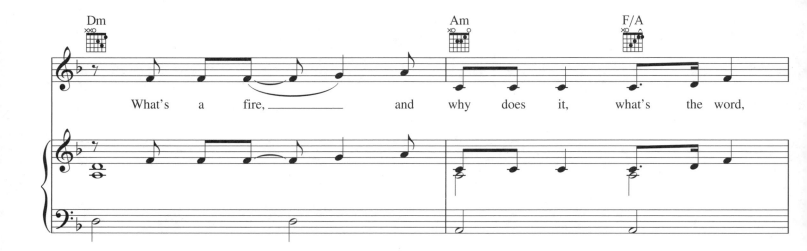

What's a fire, _____ and why does it, what's the word,

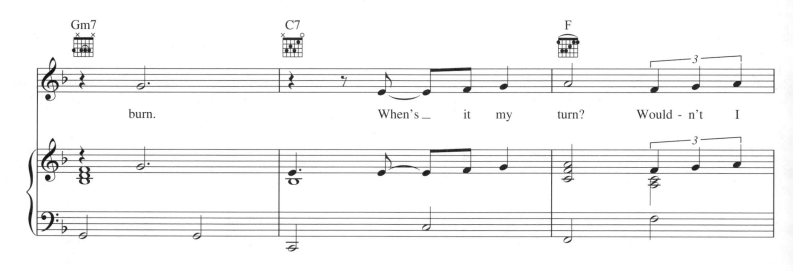

burn. When's __ it my turn? Would - n't I

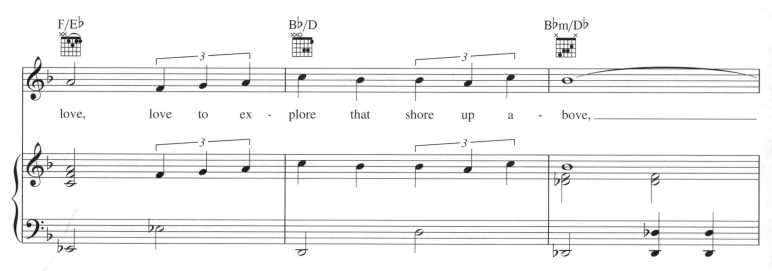

love, love to ex - plore that shore up a - bove, _____

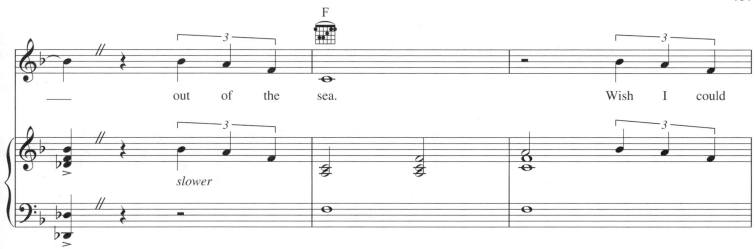

out of the sea.　　　　Wish I could

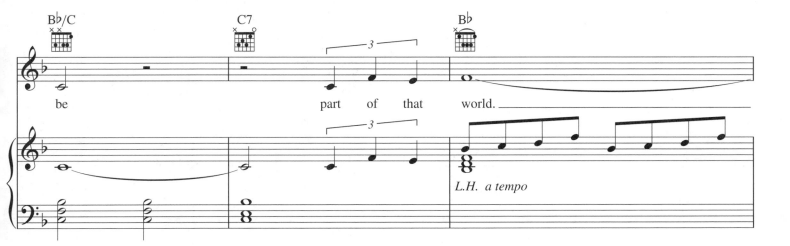

be　　　　part of that world.

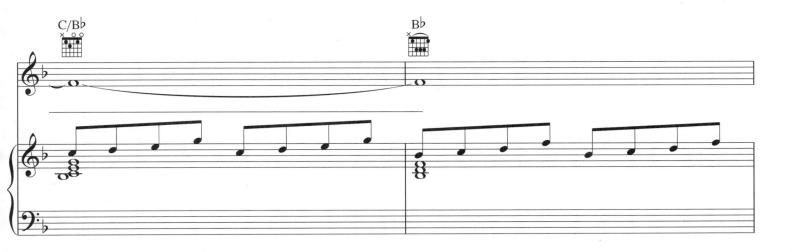

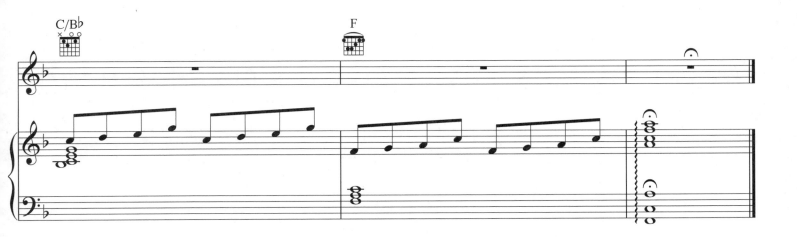

PERFECT WORLD

from Walt Disney Pictures' THE EMPEROR'S NEW GROOVE

Lyrics by STING
Music by STING and DAVID HARTLEY

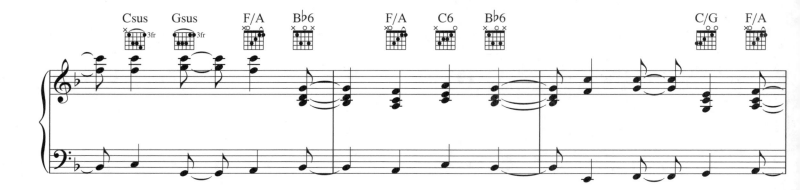

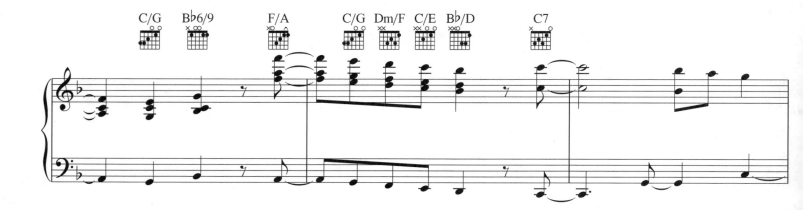

There are des - pots and dic - ta - tors, po - lit - i - cal

__ ma - nip - u - la - tors; there are blue bloods with the in -

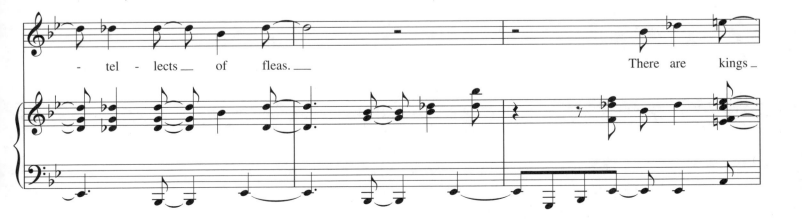

- tel - lects _ of fleas. __ There are kings _

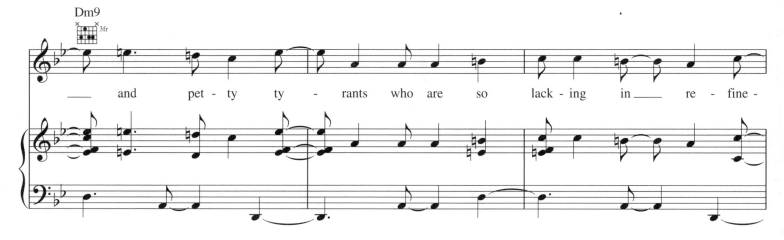

_____ and pet - ty ty - rants who are so lack-ing in _____ re - fine -

- ments, they'd be bet - ter suit - ed swing-ing from the trees.

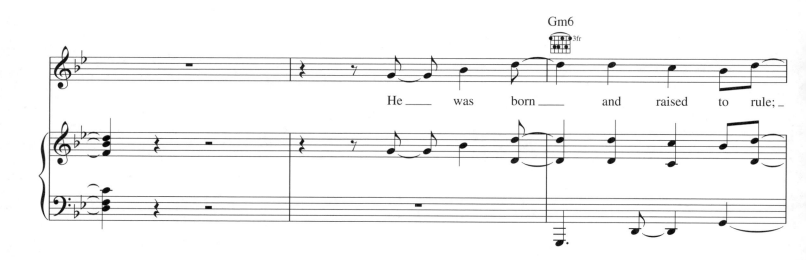

He _____ was born _____ and raised to rule; _

_____ no one has ev - er been _ this cool _____ in a

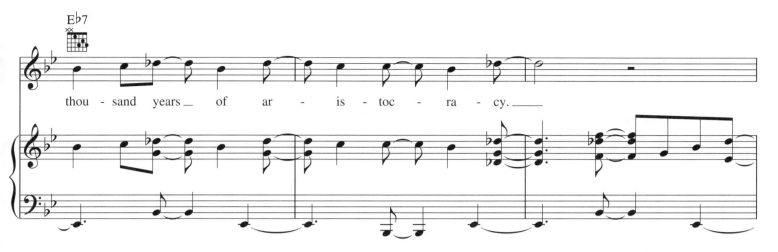

thou - sand years__ of ar - is - toc - ra - cy.___

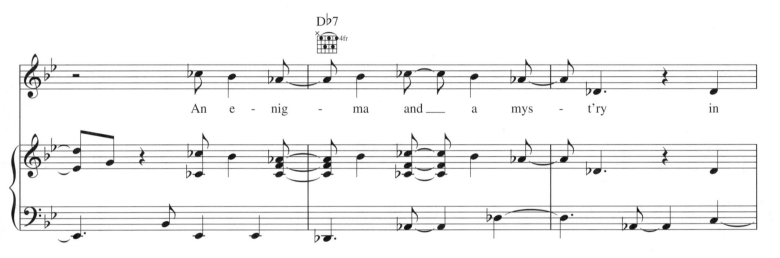

An e - nig - ma and__ a mys - t'ry in

Me - so - A - mer - i - can his - t'ry, the quin - tes - sence of__ per - fec -

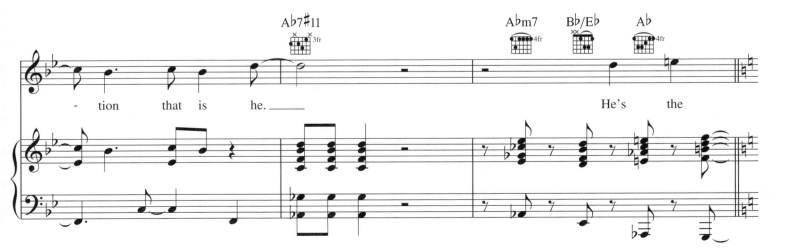

- tion that is he.___ He's the

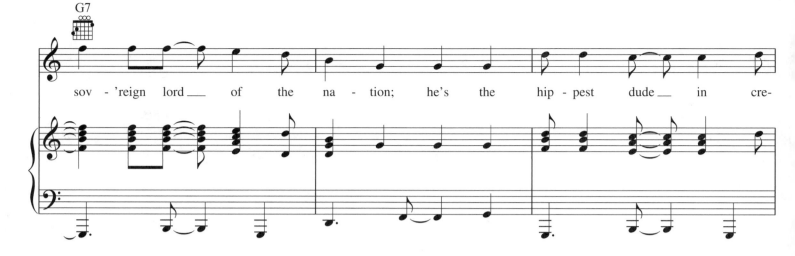

sov - 'reign lord ___ of the na - tion; he's the hip - pest dude ___ in cre-

a - tion; He's a hep cat in the em - per - or's ___ new

clothes. ___ Years of such se - lec - tive breed-

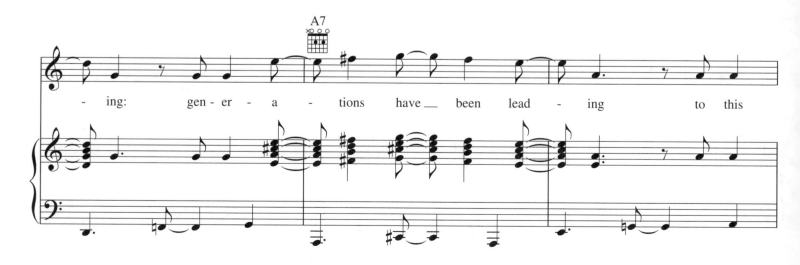

-ing: gen - er - a - tions have ___ been lead - ing to this

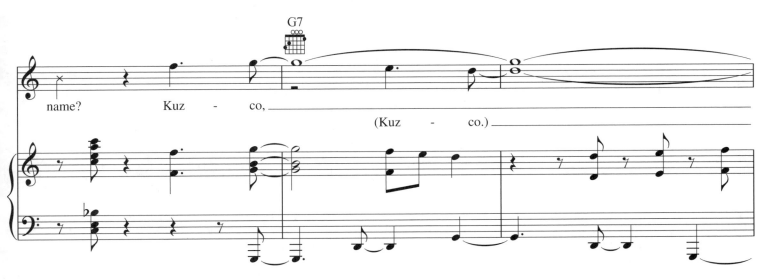

Is he hip, ___ or
(Kuz - co.) _____

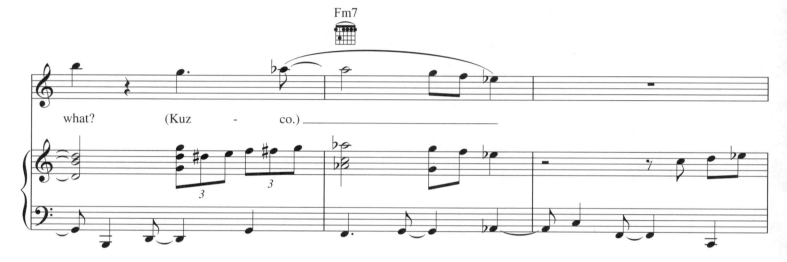

what? (Kuz - co.) _____

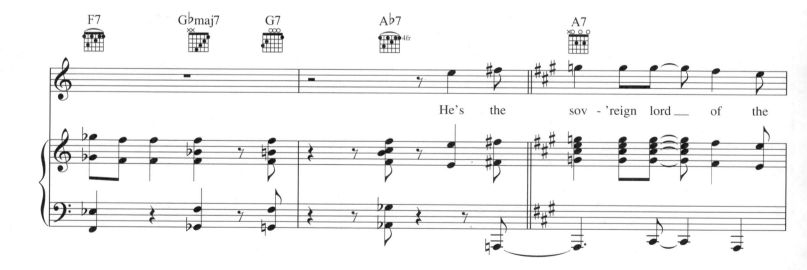

He's the sov -'reign lord ___ of the

na - tion; he's the hip -pest cat ___ in cre - a - tion; he's the

Al - pha, the O - me - ga, A___ to Z.___

And this per - fect world___ will spin a - round his ev -

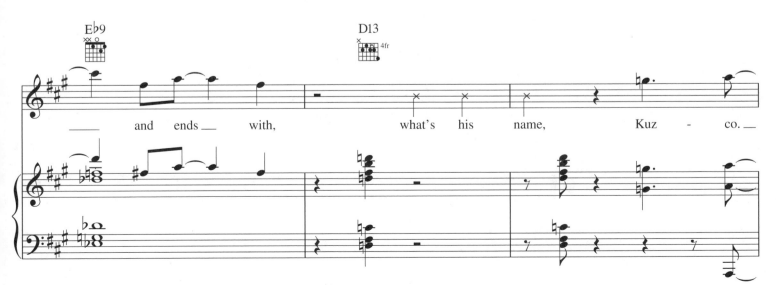

- 'ry lit - tle whim___ 'cause this per - fect world___ be - gins___

___ and ends___ with, what's his name, Kuz - co.___

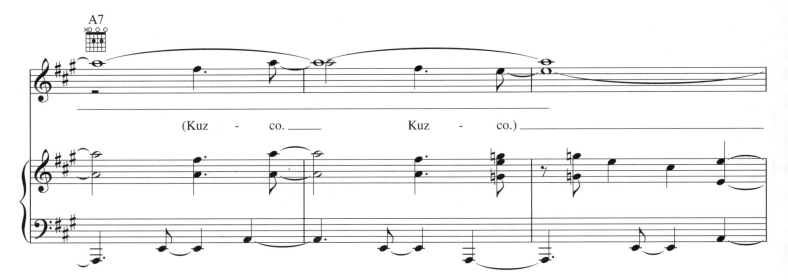

(Kuz - co. _____ Kuz - co.) _____

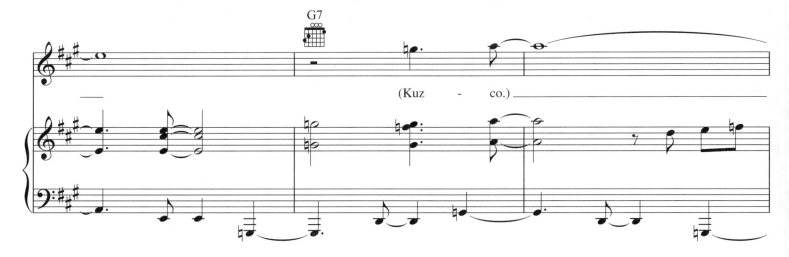

_____ (Kuz - co.) _____

_____ What's his _____ name? (Kuz - co.) _____

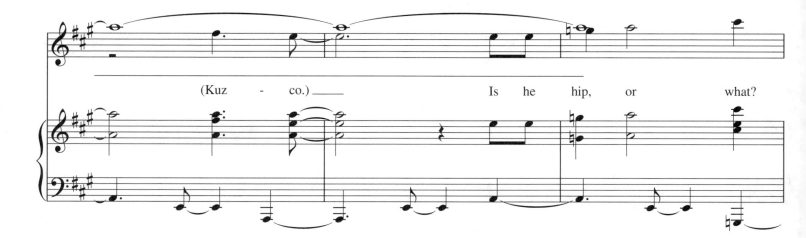

(Kuz - co.) _____ Is he hip, or what?

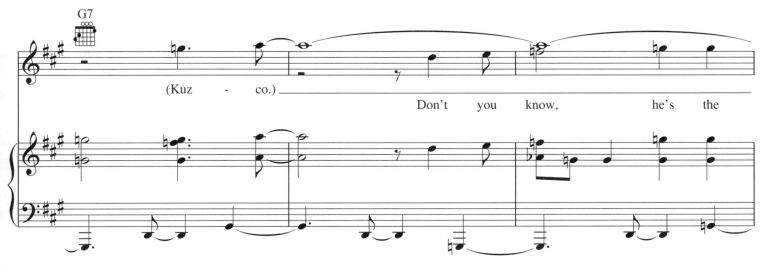

(Kuz - co.) _____ Don't you know, he's the

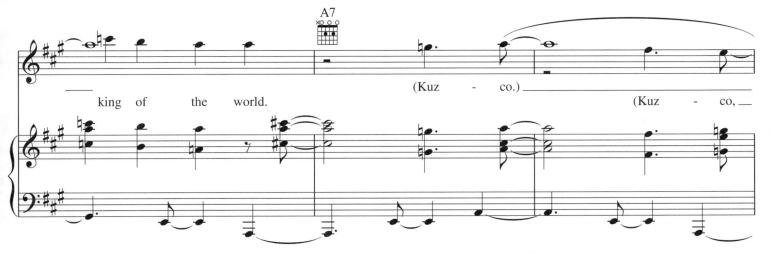

_____ king of the world. (Kuz - co.) _____ (Kuz - co, ___

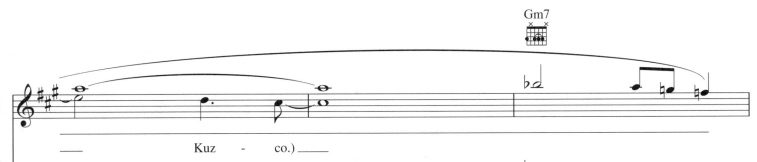

_____ Kuz - co.) _____

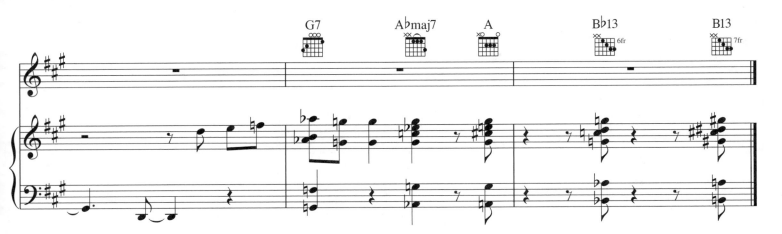

PROMISE

from MILLENNIUM CELEBRATION at Epcot

Music by GAVIN GREENAWAY
Words by DON DORSEY

Moderately slow

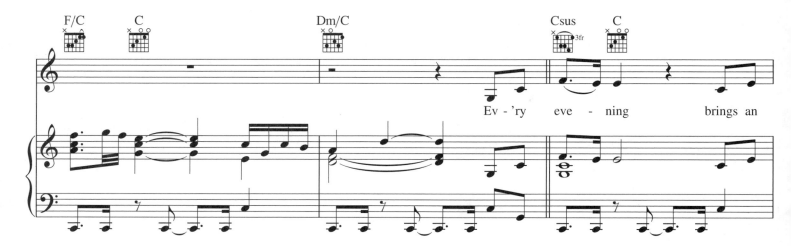

Ev-'ry eve-ning brings an

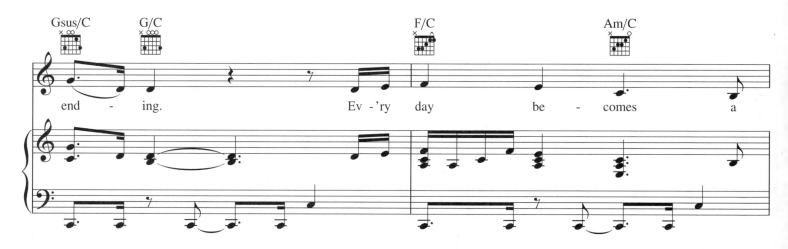

end - ing. Ev-'ry day be-comes a

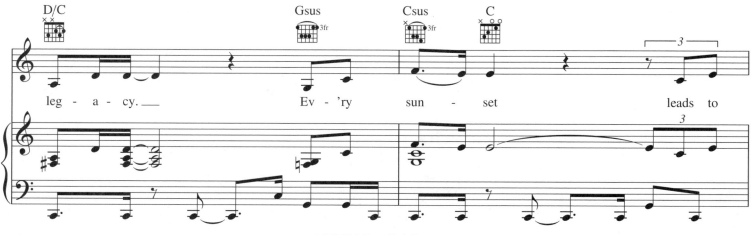

leg-a-cy. Ev-'ry sun-set leads to

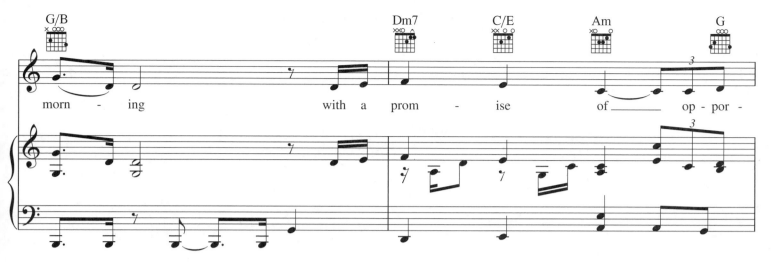

morn - ing with a prom - ise of ____ op - por -

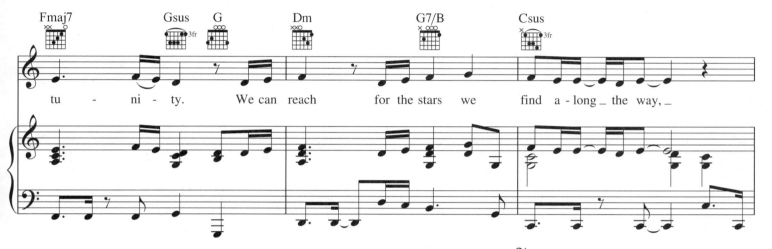

tu - ni - ty. We can reach for the stars we find a - long ___ the way, ___

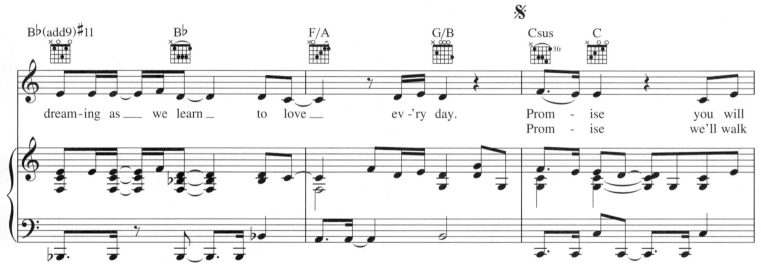

dream-ing as ___ we learn ___ to love ___ ev-'ry day. Prom - ise you will
Prom - ise we'll walk

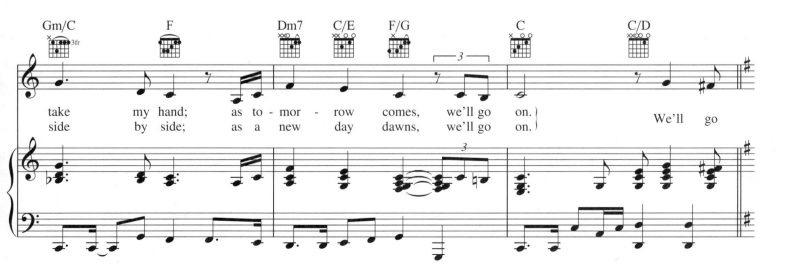

take my hand; as to - mor - row comes, we'll go on.
side by side; as a new day dawns, we'll go on. We'll go

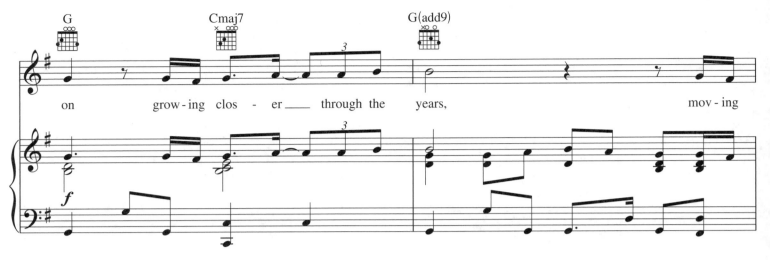

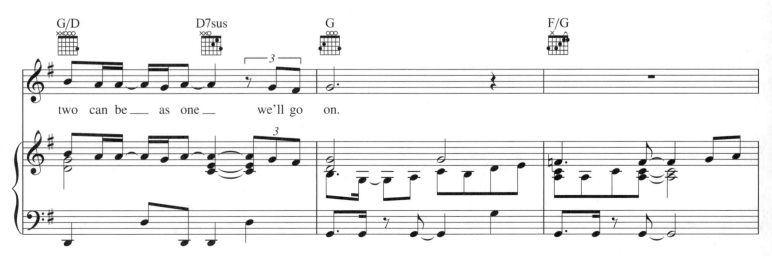

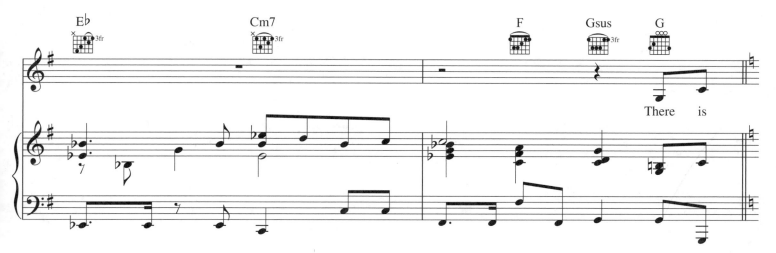

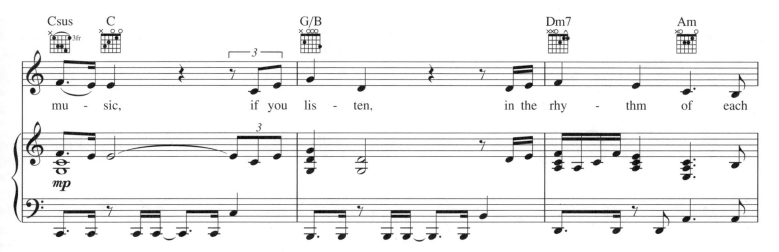

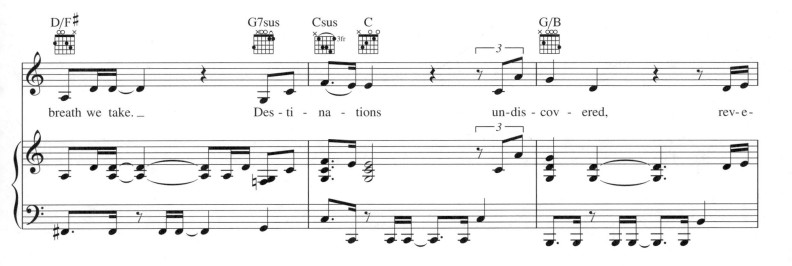

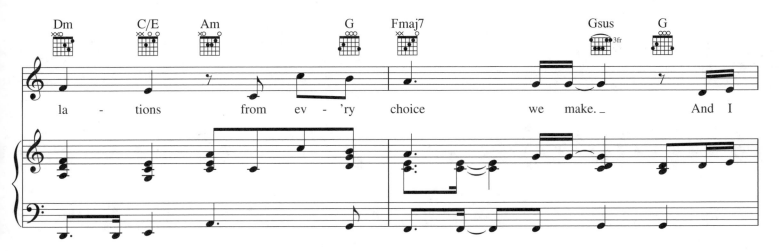

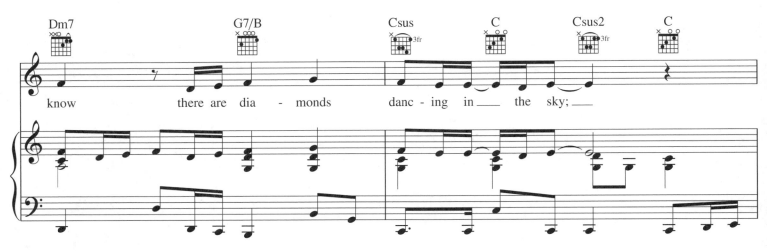

know there are dia - monds danc - ing in ___ the sky; ___

all we have ___ to do ___ is o - pen ___ our eyes. ___

D.S. al Coda

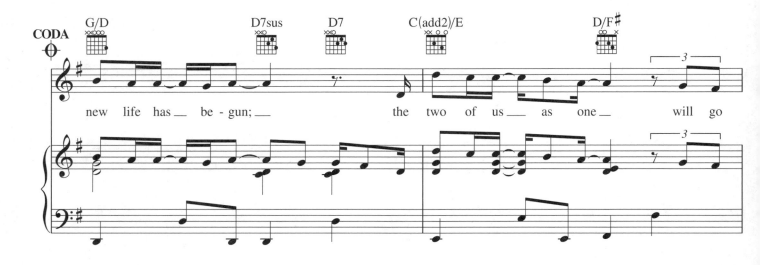

CODA

new life has ___ be - gun; ___ the two of us ___ as one ___ will go

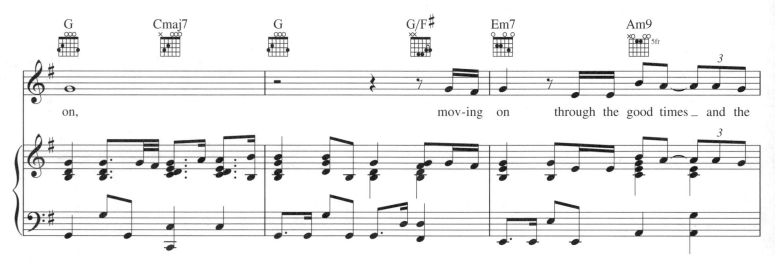

on, mov - ing on through the good times ___ and the

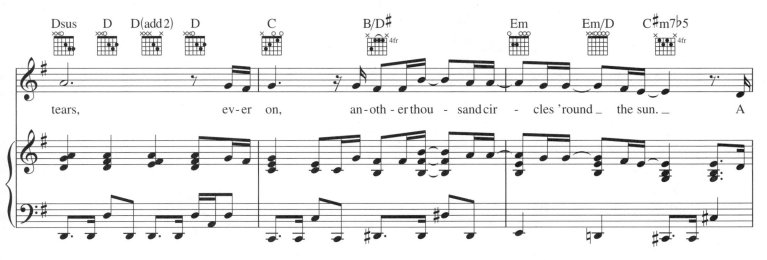

tears, ev-er on, an-oth-er thou-sand cir - cles 'round the sun. A

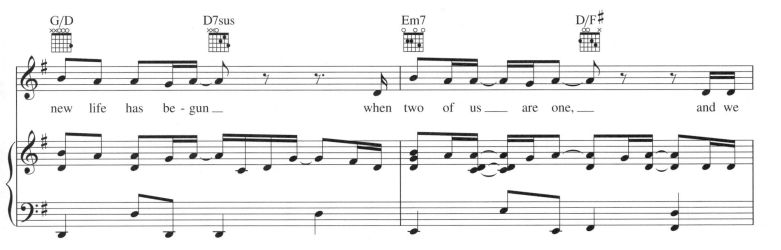

new life has be-gun when two of us are one, and we

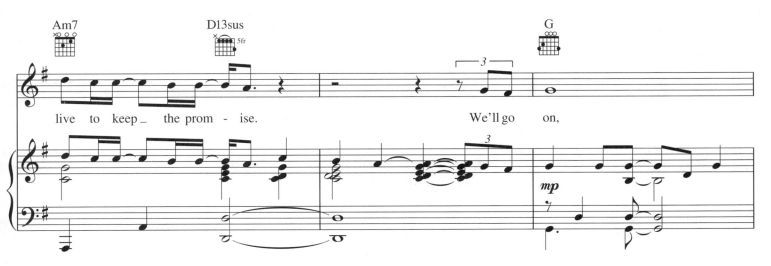

live to keep the prom - ise. We'll go on,

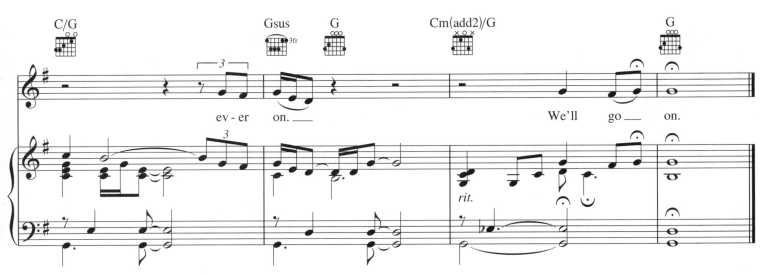

ev-er on. We'll go on.

REFLECTION
from Walt Disney Pictures' MULAN

Music by MATTHEW WILDER
Lyrics by DAVID ZIPPEL

Moderately slow

Look at me, you may think you see ___ who I ___

___ real-ly am, ___ but you'll nev-er know me. Ev-'ry day it's

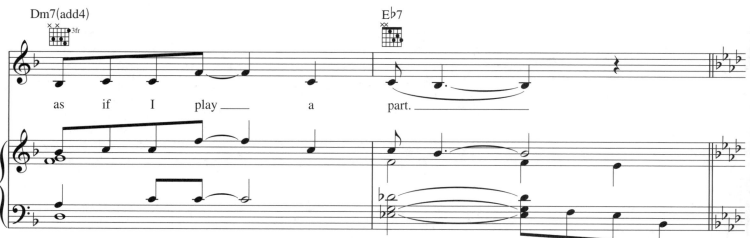

as if I play ___ a part. ___

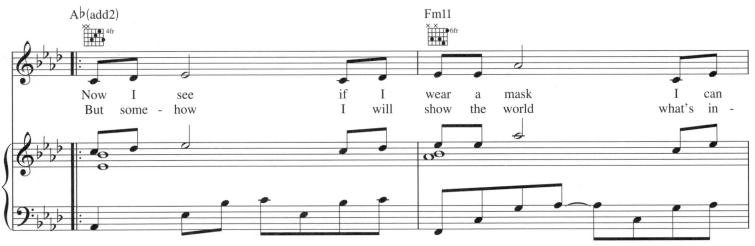

A♭(add2)   Fm11

Now I see   if I wear a mask   I can
But some - how   I will show the world   what's in -

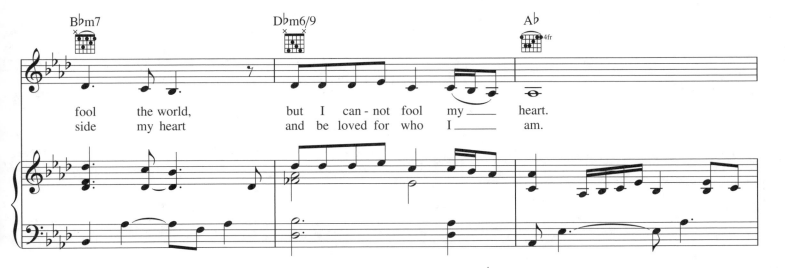

B♭m7   D♭m6/9   A♭

fool   the world,   but I can - not fool my ____ heart.
side   my heart   and be loved for who I ____ am.

A♭

Who   is that
Who   is that
(D.S.) Why   must we

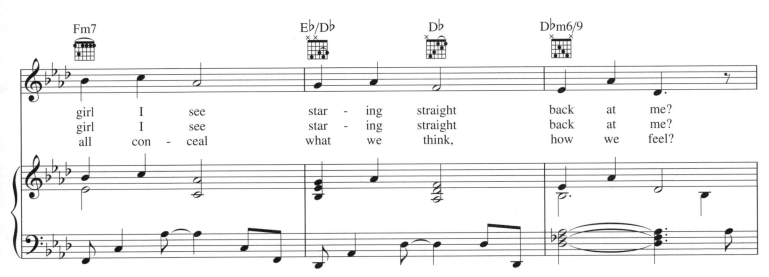

Fm7   E♭/D♭   D♭   D♭m6/9

girl I see   star - ing straight   back at me?
girl I see   star - ing straight   back at me?
all con - ceal   what we think,   how we feel?

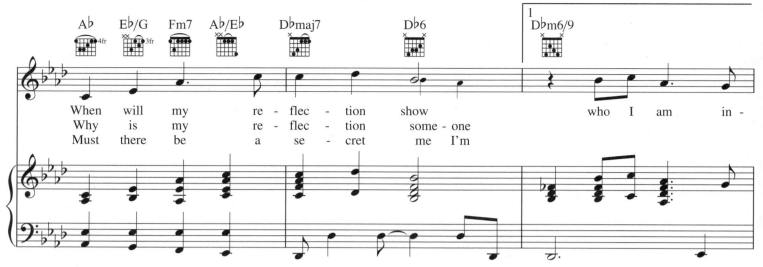

When will my re-flec-tion show who I am in-
Why is my re-flec-tion some-one
Must there be a se-cret me I'm

side? I am now in a

world where I___ have to hide my heart_ and what I be-lieve in.

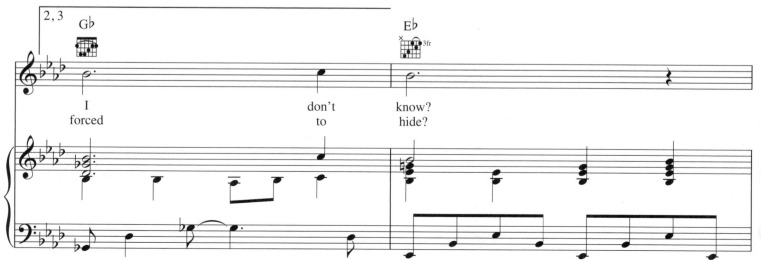

I don't know?
forced to hide?

Must I pre-tend that I'm some-one else
I won't pre-tend that I'm some-one else

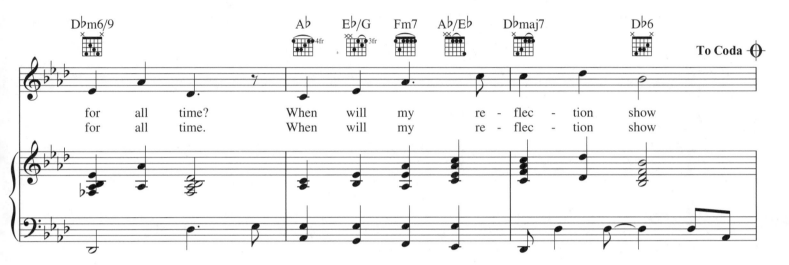

for all time? When will my re-flec-tion show
for all time. When will my re-flec-tion show

To Coda ⊕

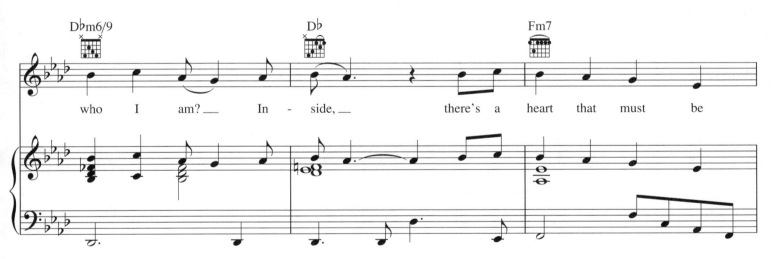

who I am? __ In - side, __ there's a heart that must be

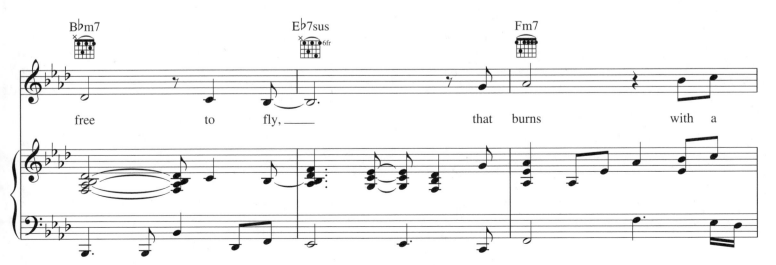

free to fly, ____ that burns with a

D.S. al Coda
(take 2nd ending)

need to know the rea - son _____ why. ___

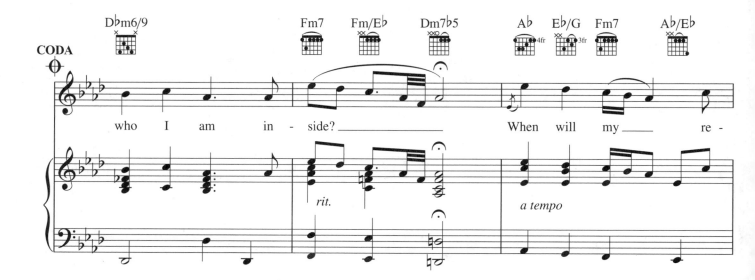

CODA

who I am in - side? _____ When will my ___ re-

rit.   *a tempo*

flec - tion show   who I am ___ in - side? _____

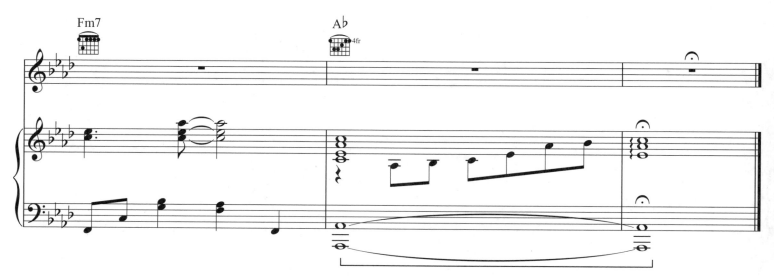

REMEMBER THE MAGIC
(Theme Song)
from Walt Disney's MUSIC FROM THE PARK CD

Lyrics and Music by IRA ANTELIS,
CHERYL BERMAN and DAVID PACK

Moderately slow, half-time feel

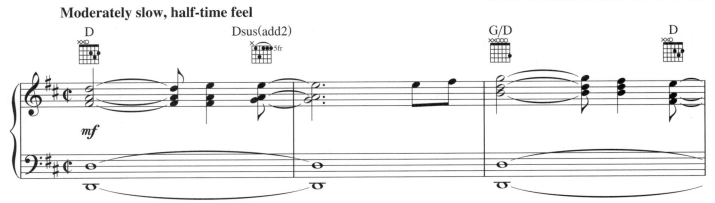

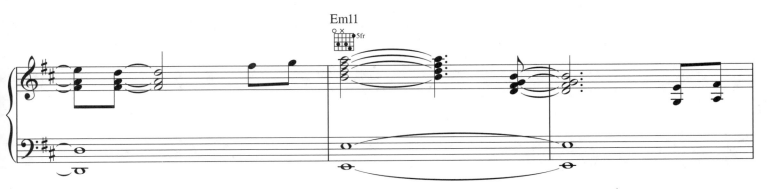

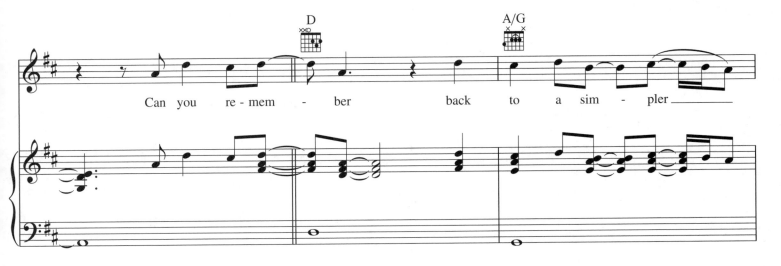

Can you re-mem - ber back to a sim - pler

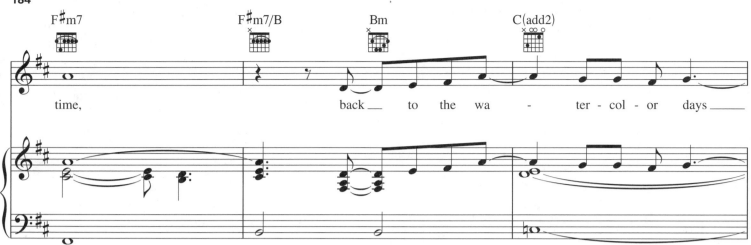

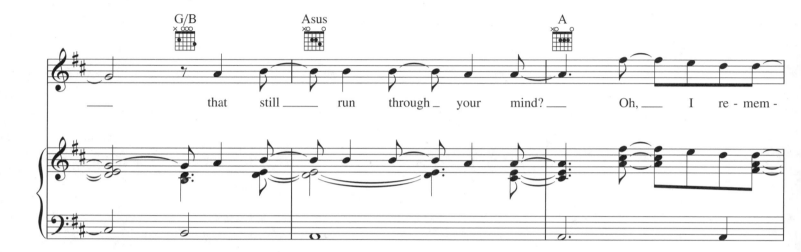

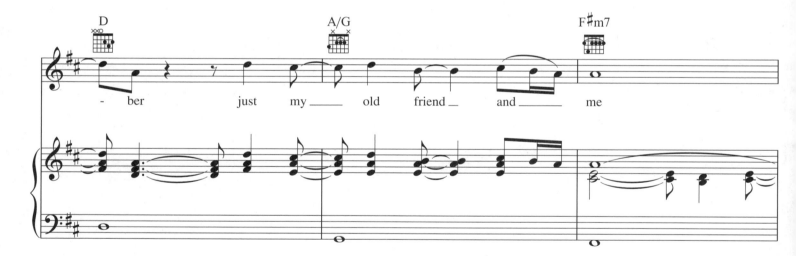

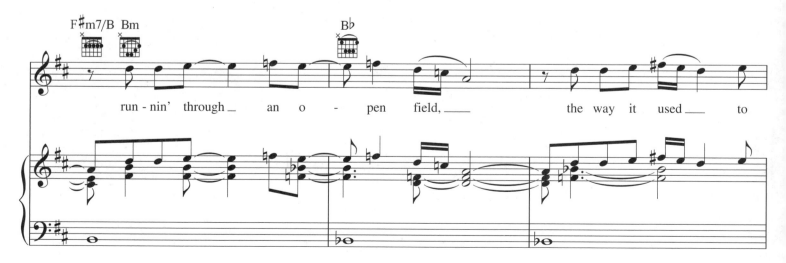

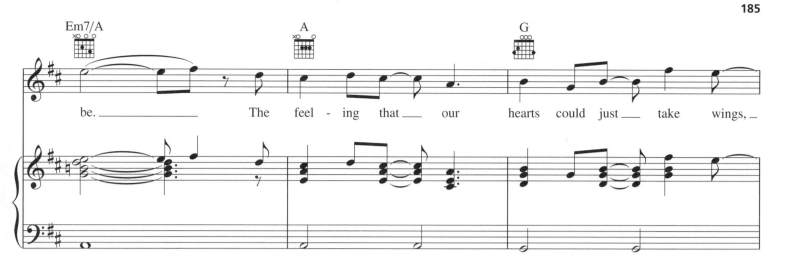

be. _____ The feel - ing that ___ our hearts could just ___ take wings, _

___ we could live out all ___ our dreams. The

jour - ney there ___ was nev - er far _____ a - way. ___

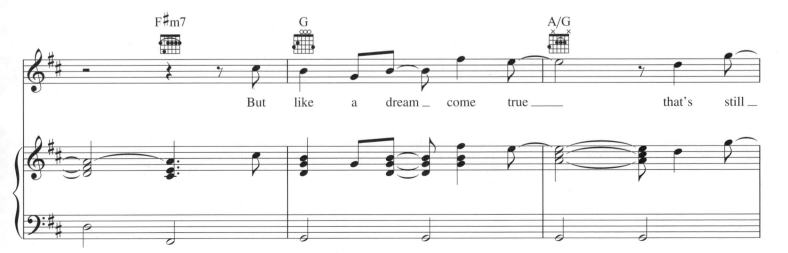

But like a dream ___ come true _____ that's still ___

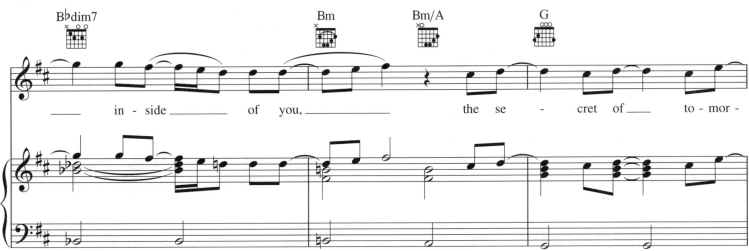

_____ in - side _____ of you, _____ the se - cret of _____ to - mor -

- row is _____ to live your dreams _____ to - day. _____

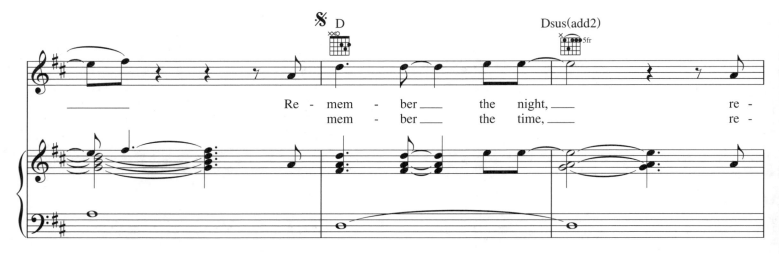

_____ Re - mem - ber _____ the night, _____ re -
mem - ber _____ the time, _____ re -

mem - ber _____ the feel - ing, _____ re - mem - ber _____ the mag -
mem - ber _____ the feel - ing, _____ re - mem - ber _____ the mag -

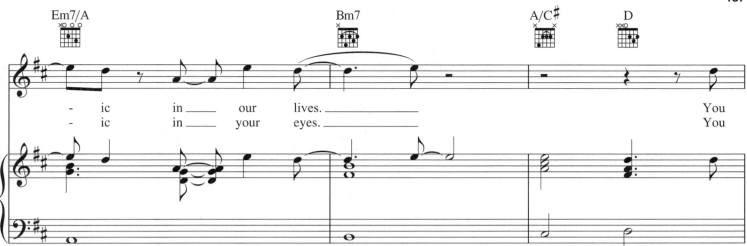

- ic in ____ our lives. _____ You
- ic in ____ your eyes. _____ You

o - pened up ____ my eyes _____ to a new world _ re - veal -
o - pened up ____ my heart, _____ and you gave life ____ new mean -

- ing. So re - mem - ber ____ the mag - ic, just re -
- ing. So re - mem - ber ____ that feel - ing, just re -

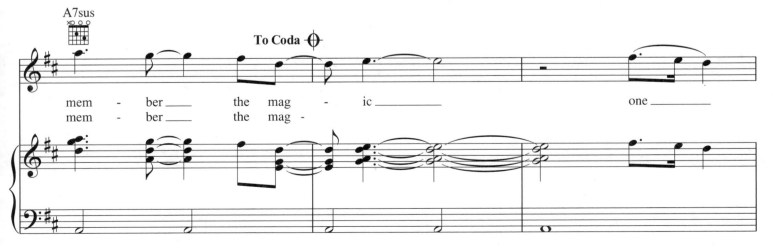

mem - ber ____ the mag - ic _____ one _____
mem - ber ____ the mag -

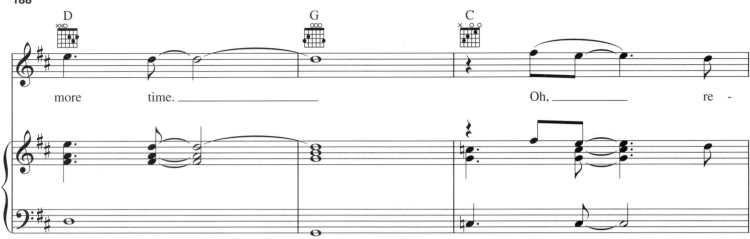

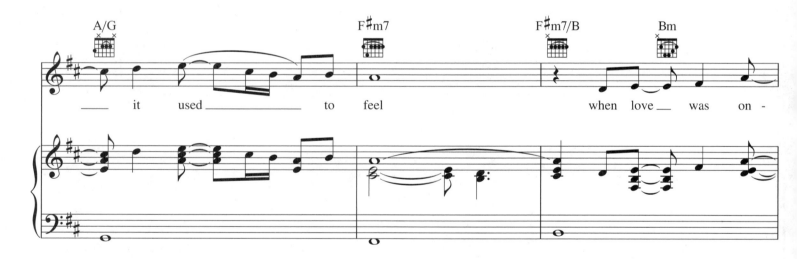

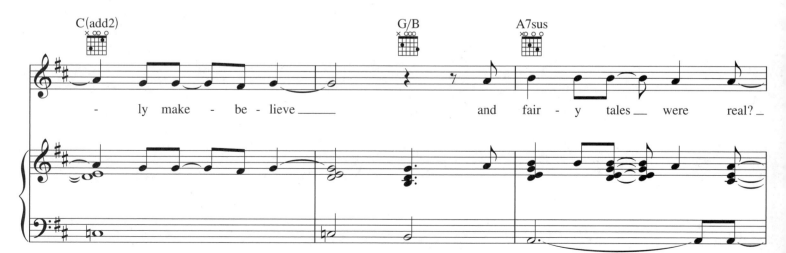

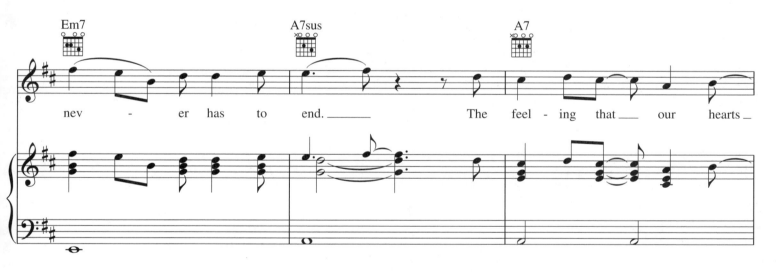

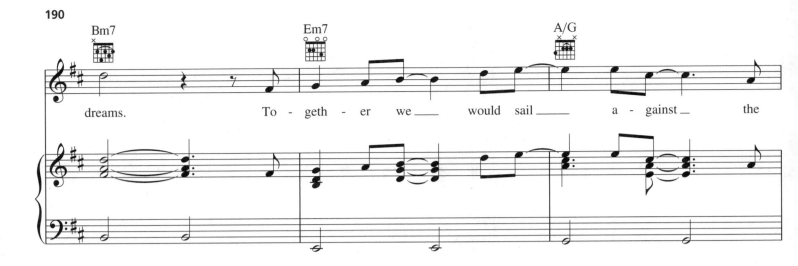

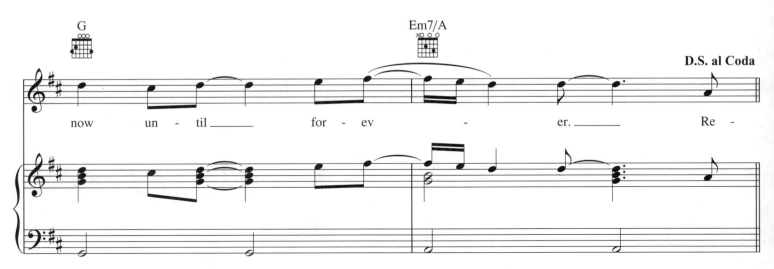

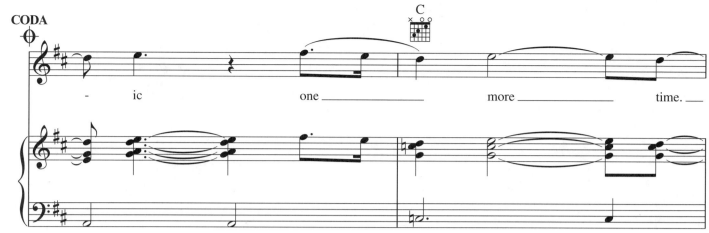

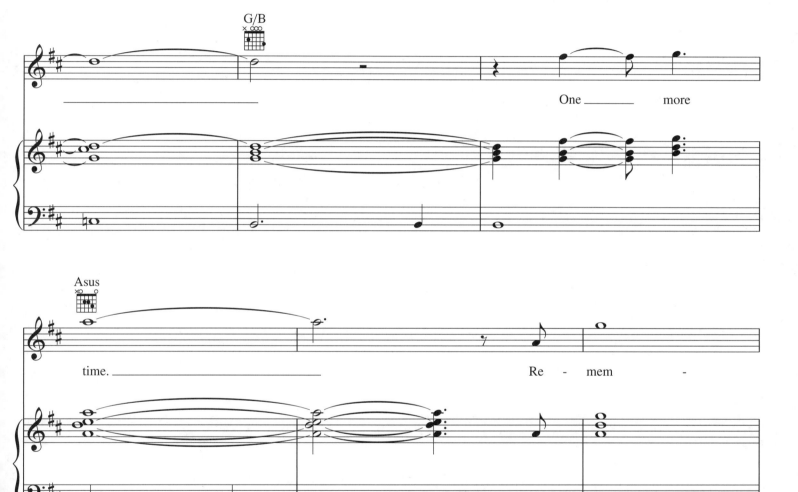

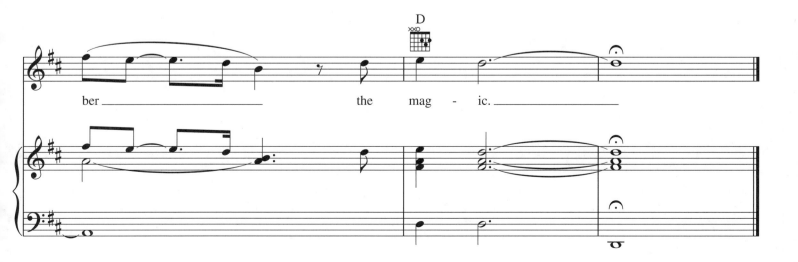

ROCK STAR

Words and Music by JEANNIE LURIE,
ARIS ARCHONTIS and CHEN NEEMAN

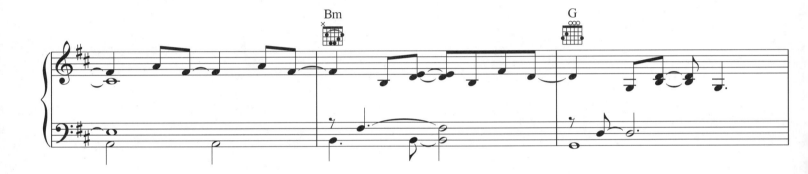

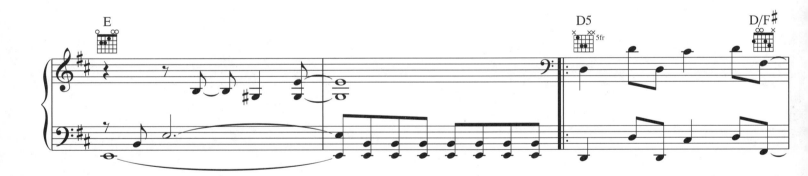

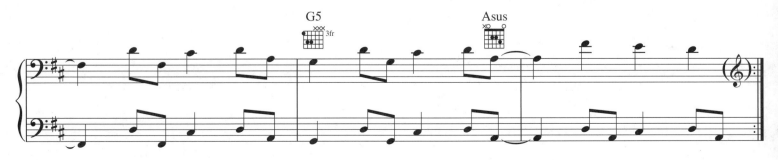

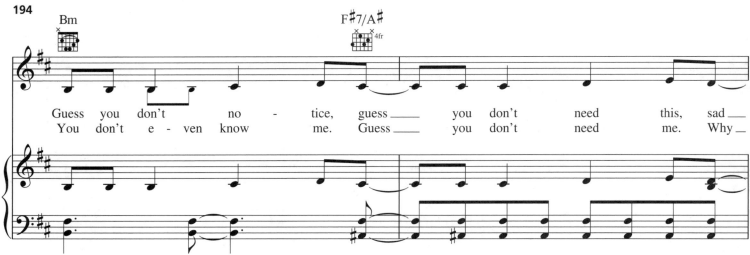

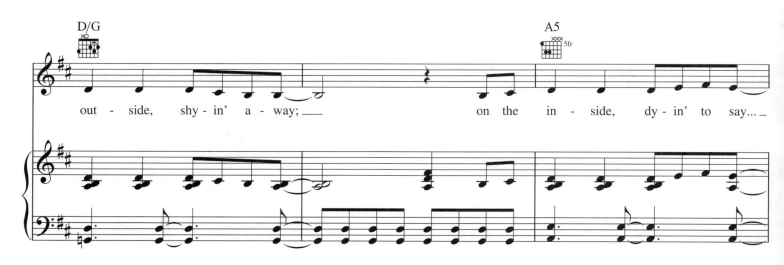

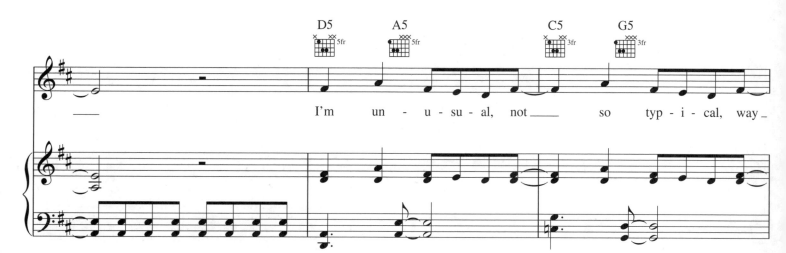

too smart to be wait - ing a - round. Tai Chi prac - tic - in', snow-

- board cham - pi - on, I could fix a flat on your car. ____ I might e - ven be a

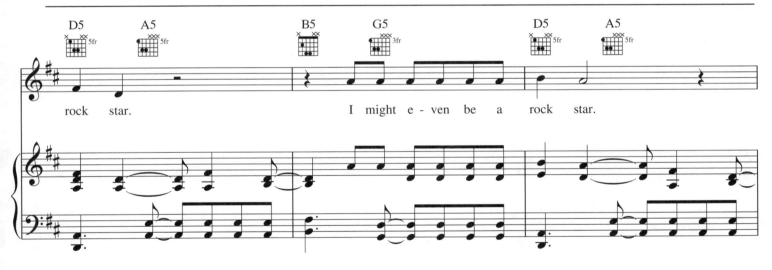

rock star. I might e - ven be a rock star.

____ I might e - ven be a rock star.

If you on-ly knew ___ the ___ real me... ___ I might e-ven be a

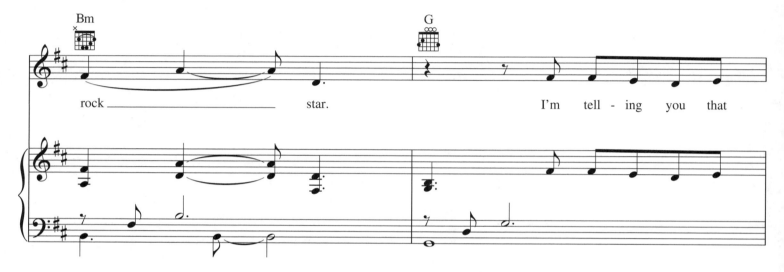

rock _____ star. I'm tell-ing you that

we are meant ___ to be, _____ that would-n't it be

nice if you ___ could see that I real-ly am a rock star,

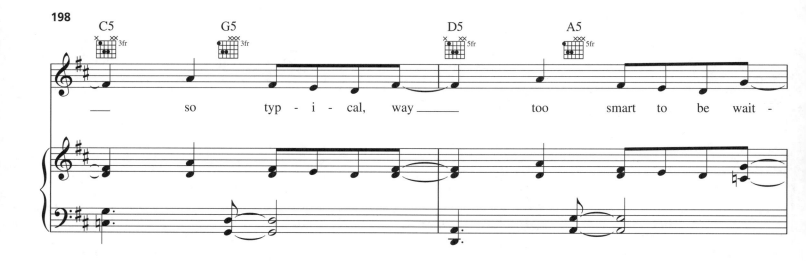

so typ - i - cal, way ____ too smart to be wait -

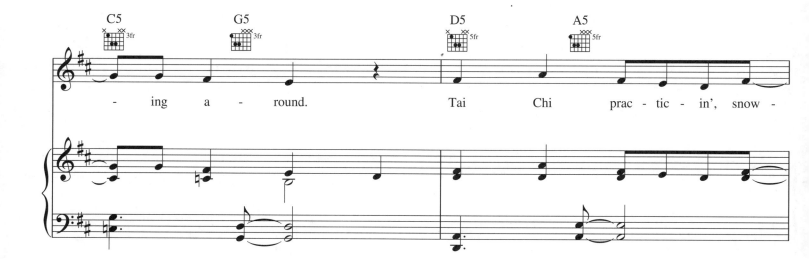

- ing a - round. Tai Chi prac - tic - in', snow -

- board cham - pi - on, I could fix a flat on your car. ___

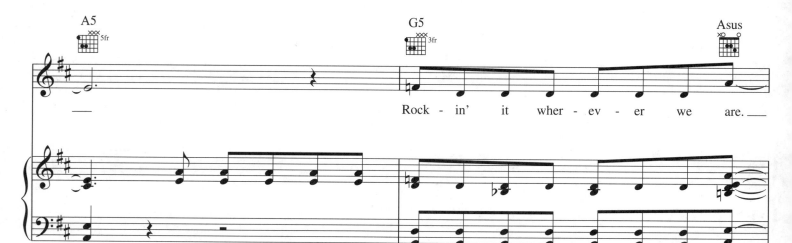

Rock - in' it wher - ev - er we are. ___

Yeah, yeah, that I real-ly am a rock star,

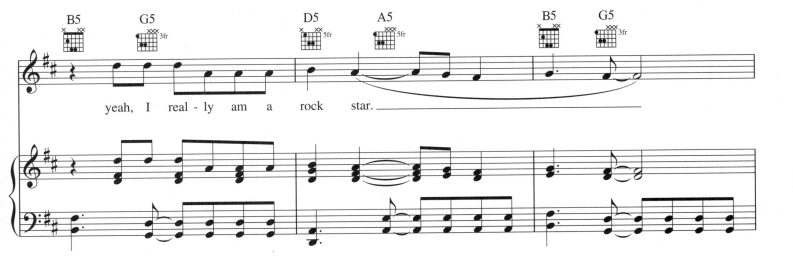

yeah, I real-ly am a rock star. _____

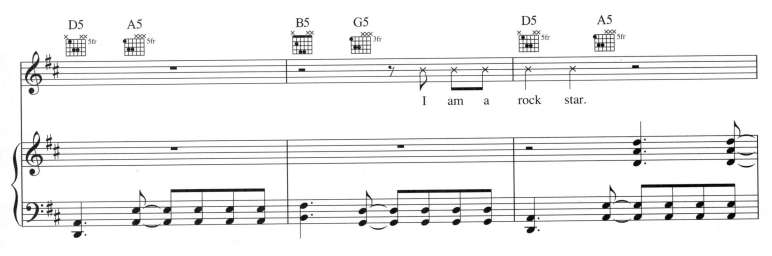

I am a rock star.

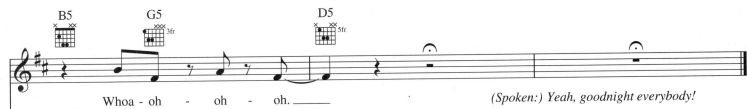

Whoa-oh - oh - oh. _____

(Spoken:) Yeah, goodnight everybody!

SEIZE THE DAY
from Walt Disney's NEWSIES

Lyrics by JACK FELDMAN
Music by ALAN MENKEN

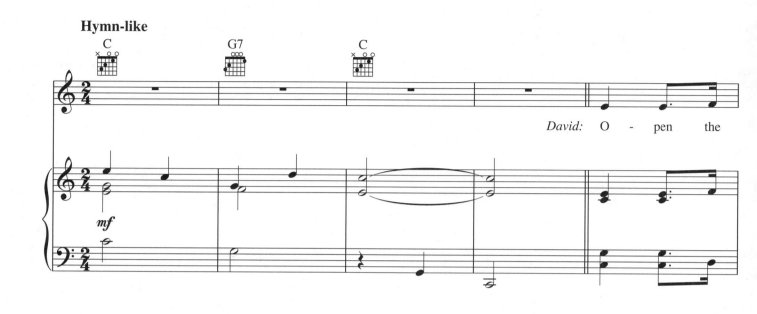

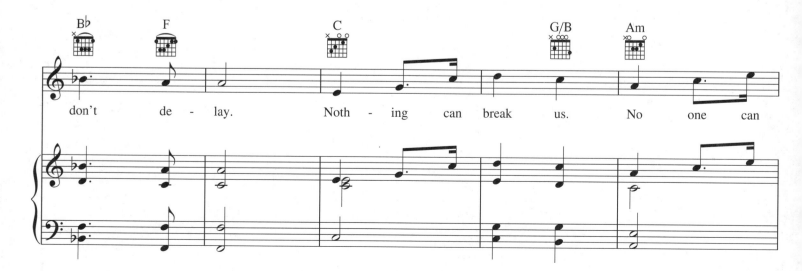

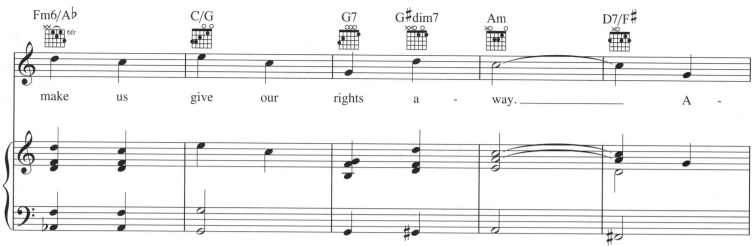

make us give our rights a - way. _____ A -

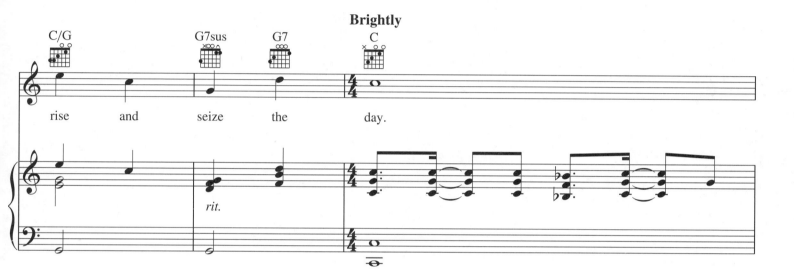

Brightly

rise and seize the day.

rit.

David: Now is the time to seize the day.

Newsies:
(Now is the time to seize the day.) David: Send out the call and join the fray.

Newsies:
(Send out the call and join the fray.) David: Wrongs will __ be right - ed

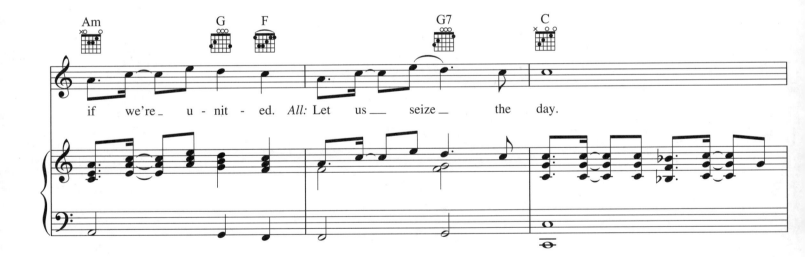

if we're __ u - nit - ed. All: Let us __ seize __ the day.

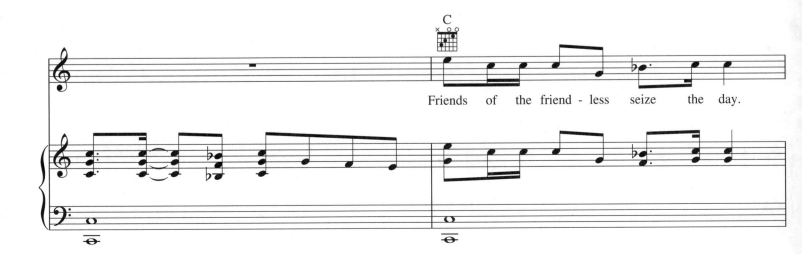

Friends of the friend - less seize the day.

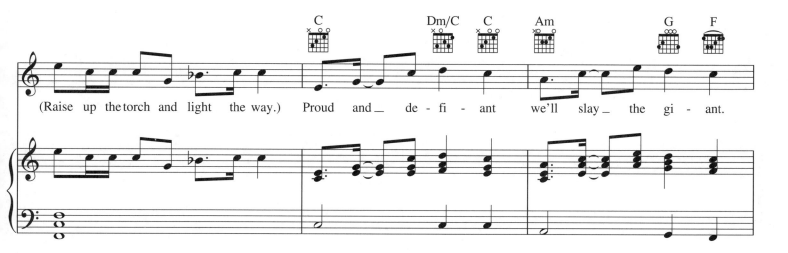

(Friends of the friend - less, seize the day.) Raise up the torch and light the way.

(Raise up the torch and light the way.) Proud and__ de - fi - ant we'll slay__ the gi - ant.

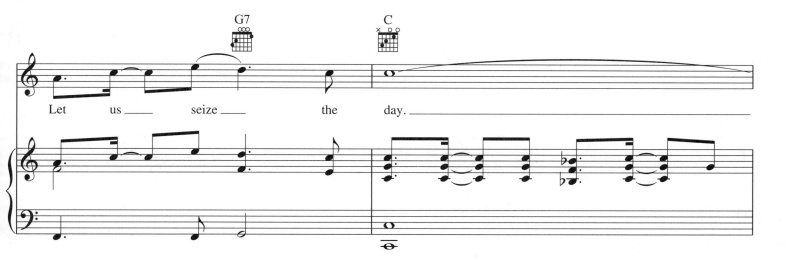

Let us____ seize____ the day.____

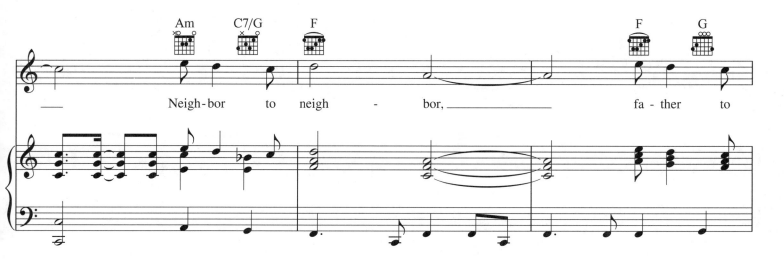

Neigh - bor to neigh - bor,_____ fa - ther to

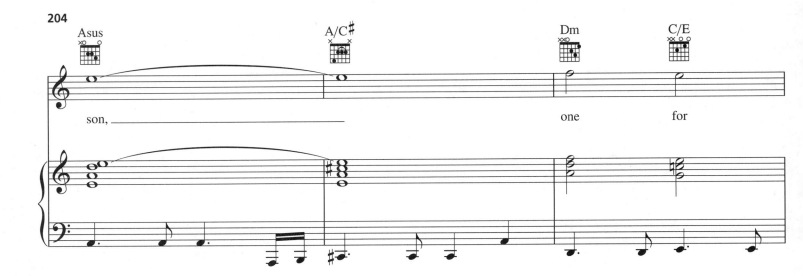

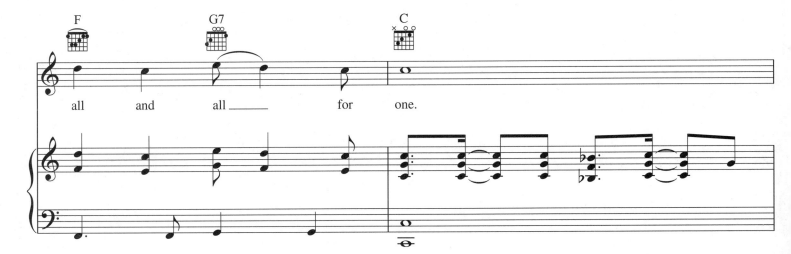

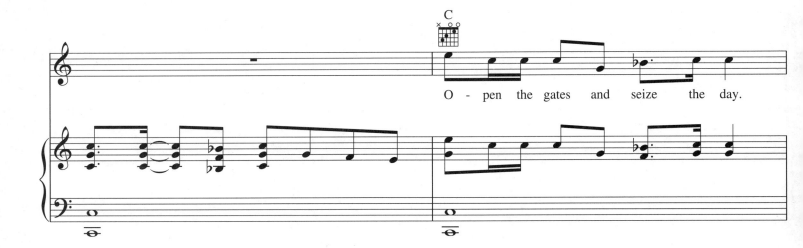

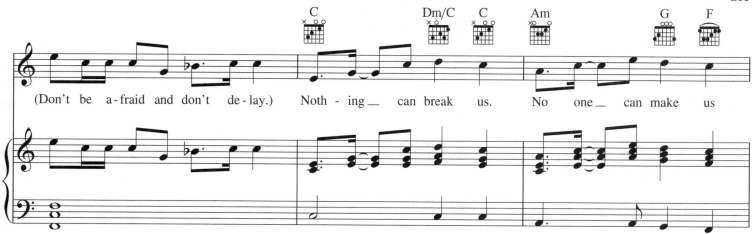

(Don't be a-fraid and don't de-lay.) Noth-ing __ can break us. No one __ can make us

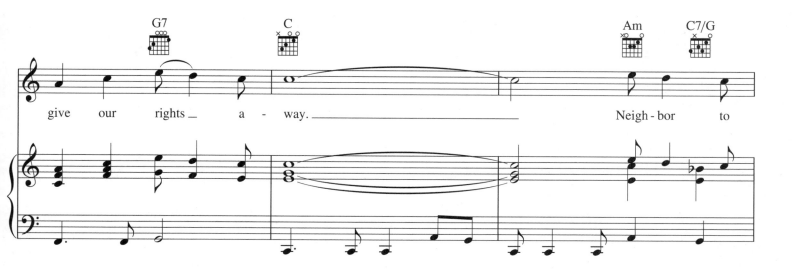

give our rights __ a - way. _____ Neigh-bor to

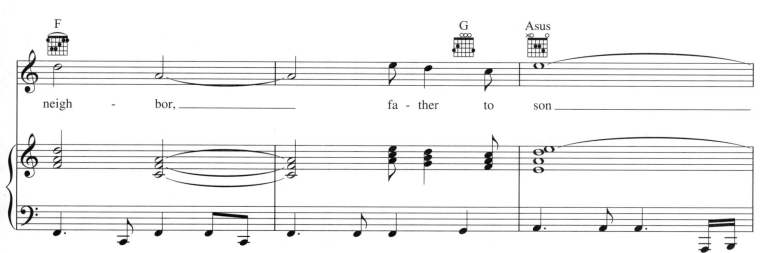

neigh - bor, _____ fa - ther to son _____

one for all and all __ for one.

SHADOWLAND

Disney Presents THE LION KING: THE BROADWAY MUSICAL

Music by LEBO M and HANS ZIMMER
Lyrics by MARK MANCINA and LEBO M

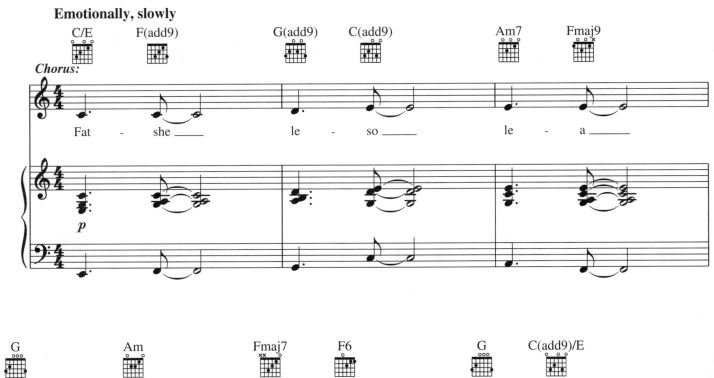

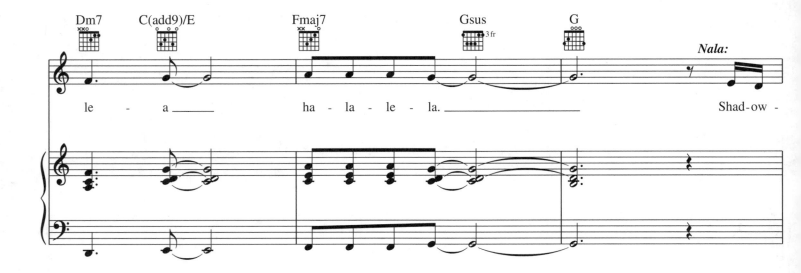

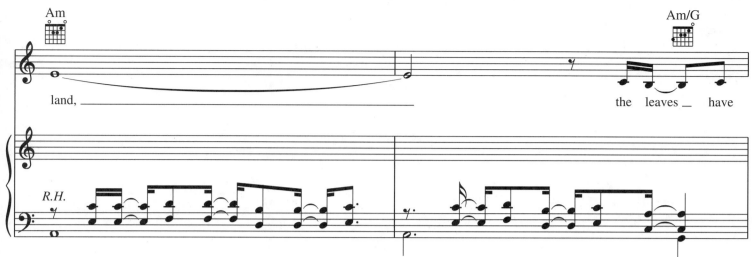

land, _____ the leaves _ have

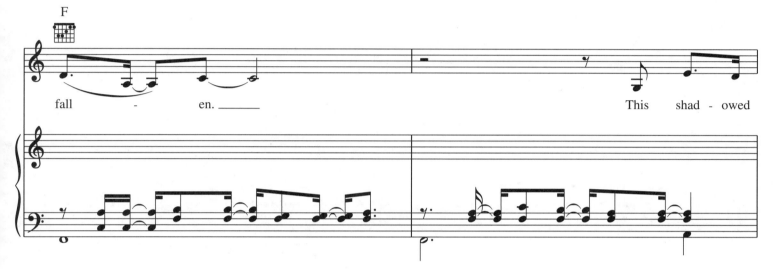

fall - en. _____ This shad - owed

land, _____ this was our

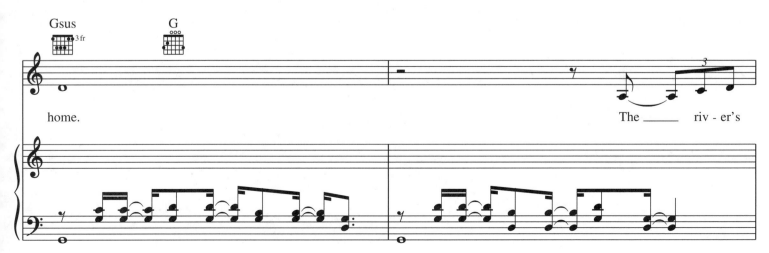

home. The _____ riv - er's

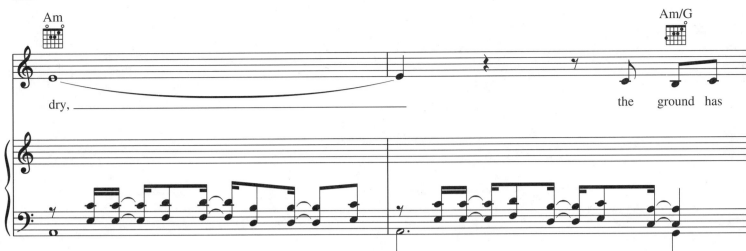

dry, _____ the ground has

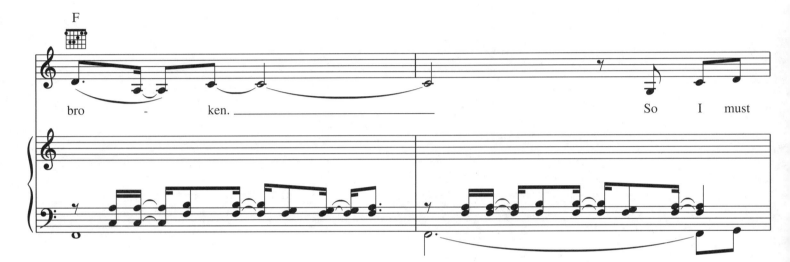

bro - ken. _____ So I must

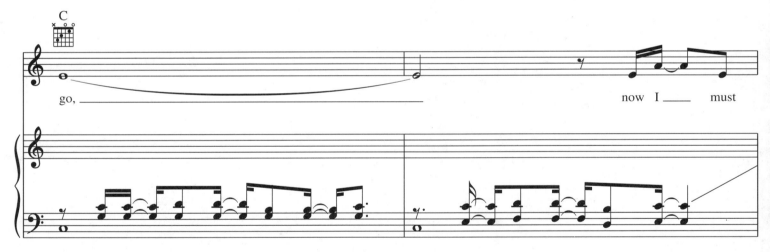

go, _____ now I ___ must

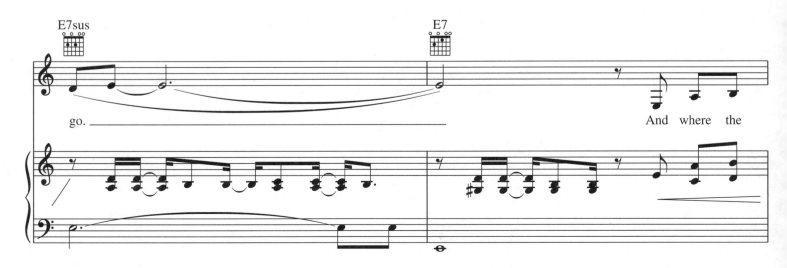

go. _____ And where the

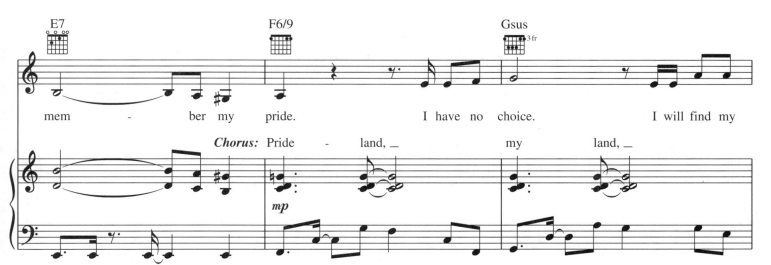

what lies out ___ there. Le - a ha - la - le - la. ___

with you, ___ fat - she ___ le - so. ___

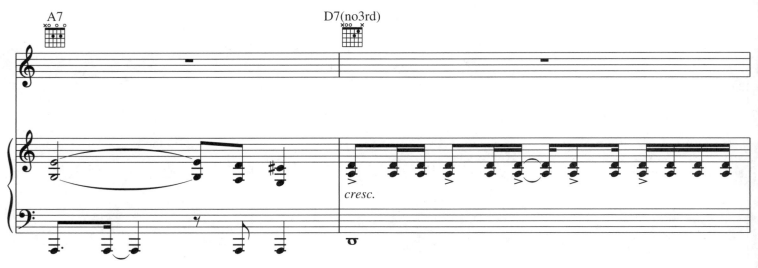

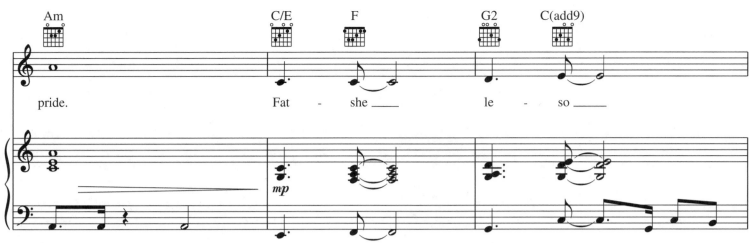

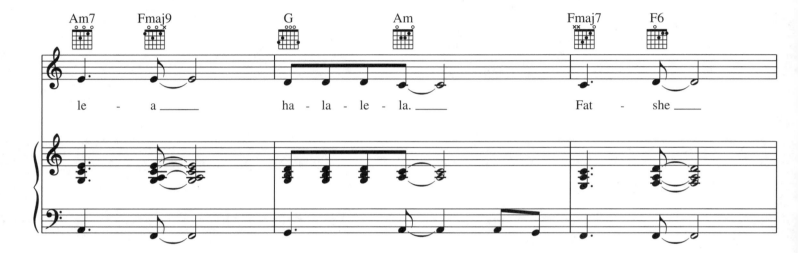

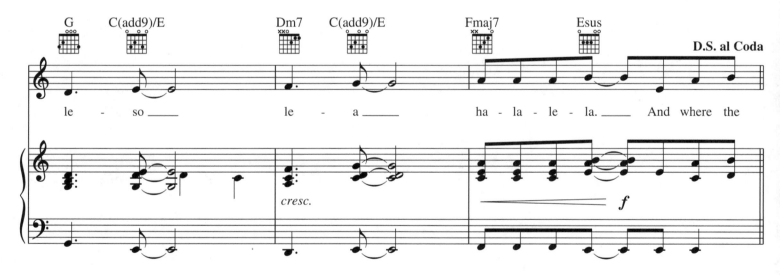

SOMEDAY

from Walt Disney's THE HUNCHBACK OF NOTRE DAME

Music by ALAN MENKEN
Lyrics by STEPHEN SCHWARTZ

on its way. Let it come some - day.

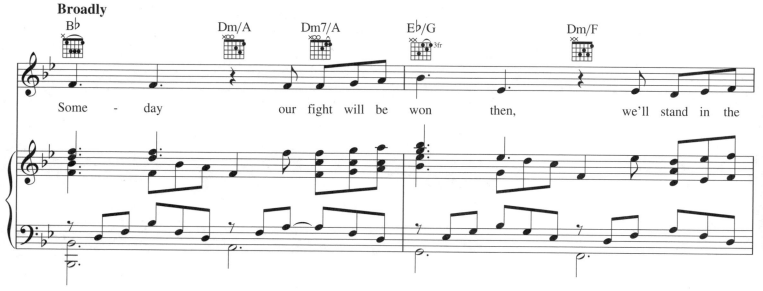

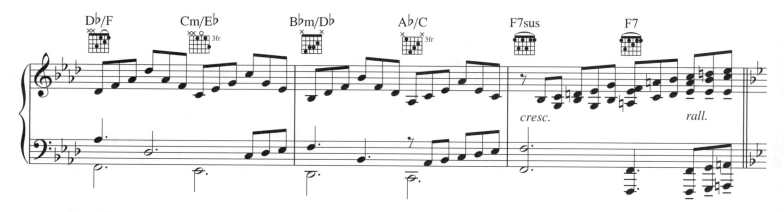

Broadly

Some - day our fight will be won then, we'll stand in the

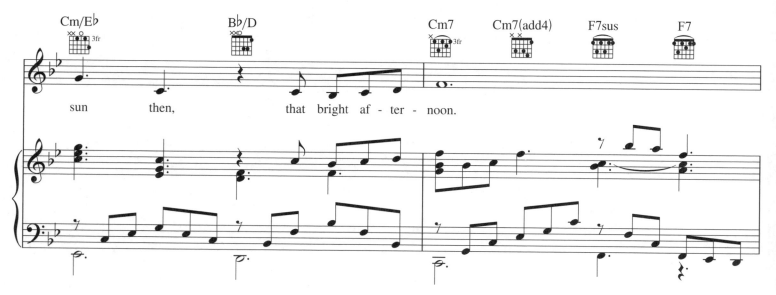

sun then, that bright af - ter - noon.

SOMETHING THERE

from Walt Disney's BEAUTY AND THE BEAST

Lyrics by HOWARD ASHMAN
Music by ALAN MENKEN

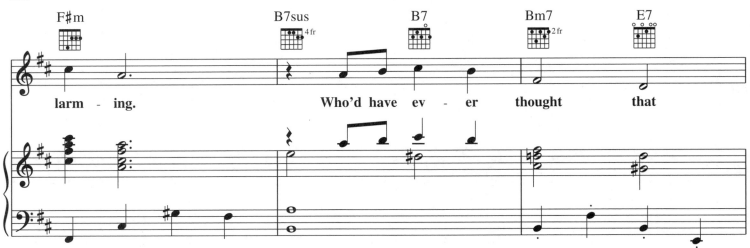

larm - ing. Who'd have ev - er thought that

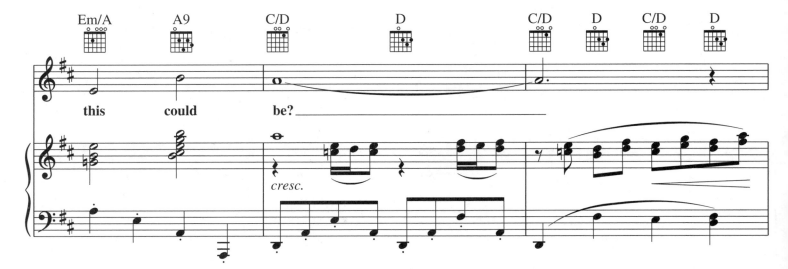

this could be? _____

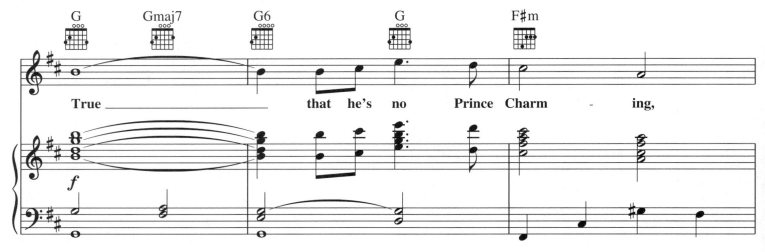

True _____ that he's no Prince Charm - ing,

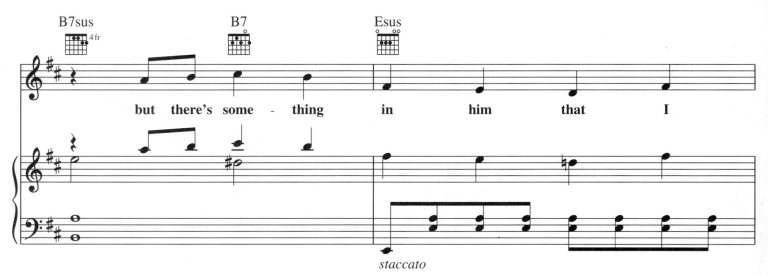

but there's some - thing in him that I

WHAT I'VE BEEN LOOKING FOR

from the Disney Channel Original Movie HIGH SCHOOL MUSICAL

Words and Music by ANDY DODD
and ADAM WATTS

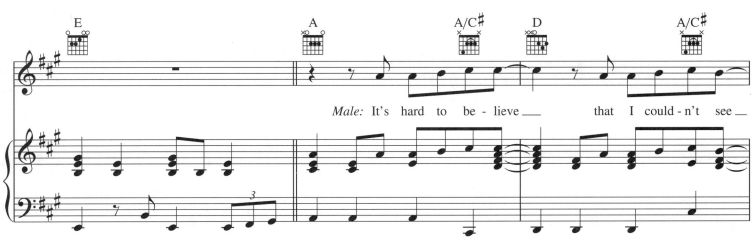

Male: It's hard to be-lieve ___ that I could-n't see ___

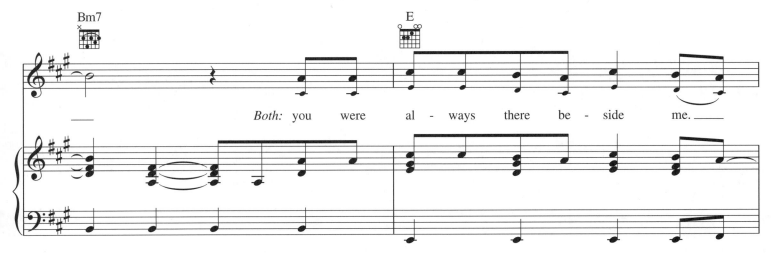

Both: you were al-ways there be-side me. ___

Thought I was a-lone, ___ with no one to hold; ___ but you were

one as good for me as you; ___ no one like you. ___

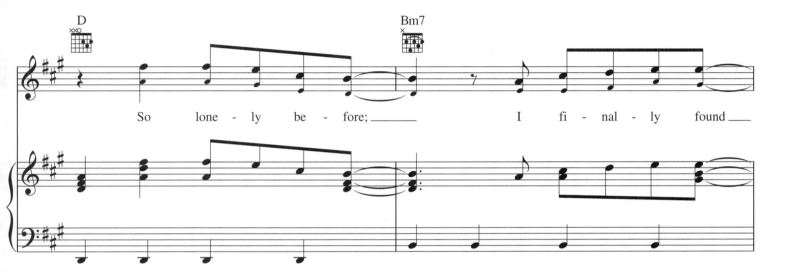

So lone - ly be - fore; ___ I fi - nal - ly found ___

To Coda ⊕

what I've been look - ing for. ___

Female: So good to be seen; _____ so good to be heard. _____ *Both:* Don't

have to say a word. _____ *Male:* For so long, I was lost; _____

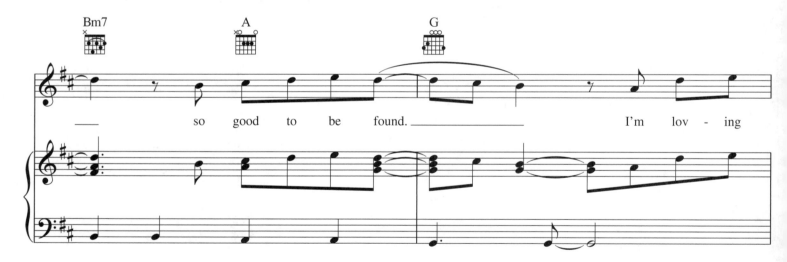

_____ so good to be found. _____ I'm lov - ing

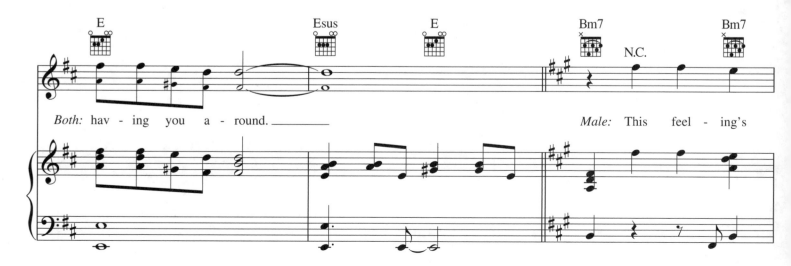

Both: hav - ing you a - round. _____ *Male:* This feel - ing's

THAT'S HOW YOU KNOW

from Walt Disney Pictures' ENCHANTED

Music by ALAN MENKEN
Lyrics by STEPHEN SCHWARTZ

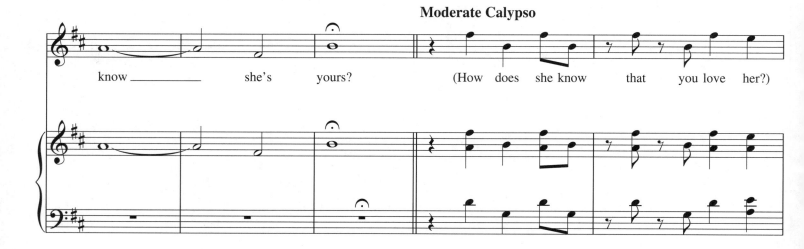

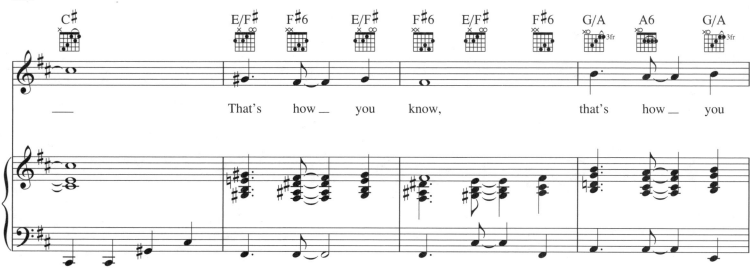

That's how _ you know, that's how _ you

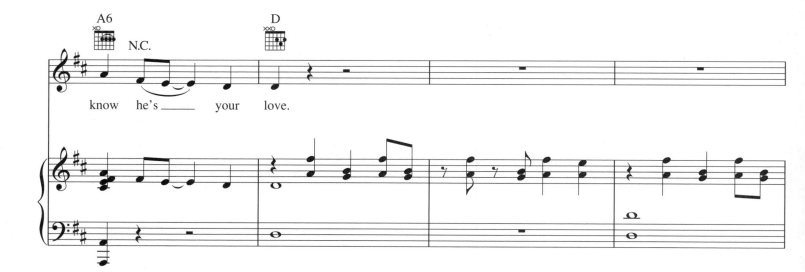

know he's ____ your love.

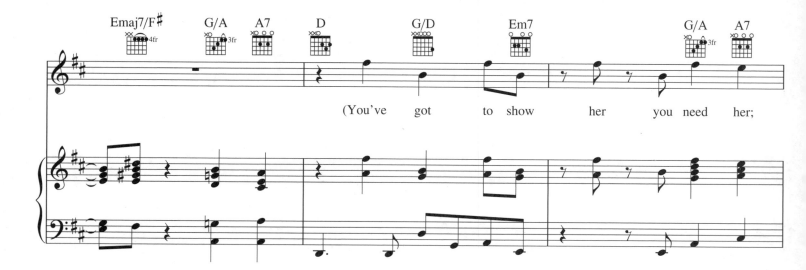

(You've got to show her you need her;

That's how you know _____
(La la la la _____ _____ he loves you. _____ la la la la, la la la la _____ la la la la. That's how you know _____

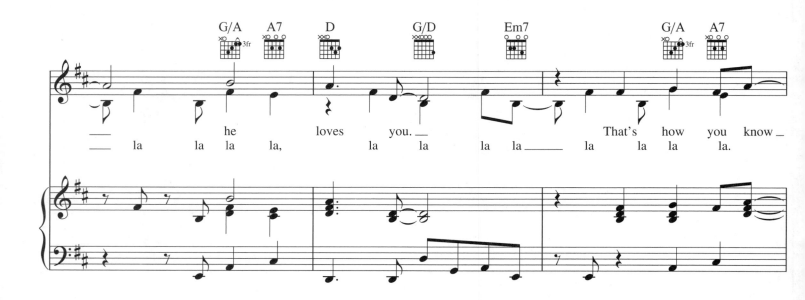

La la la la _____ la la la la la la _____ la it's true.

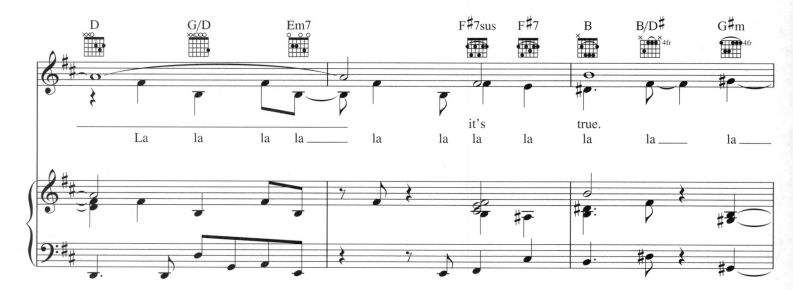

THEY LIVE IN YOU

Disney Presents THE LION KING: THE BROADWAY MUSICAL

Music and Lyrics by MARK MANCINA,
JAY RIFKIN and LEBO M

Spiritually, steadily

In - gon-ya - ma nengw' en - a - ma-ba - la.

In - gon-ya - ma nengw' en - a - ma-ba - la. Night

and the spir - it ___ of life call - ing.

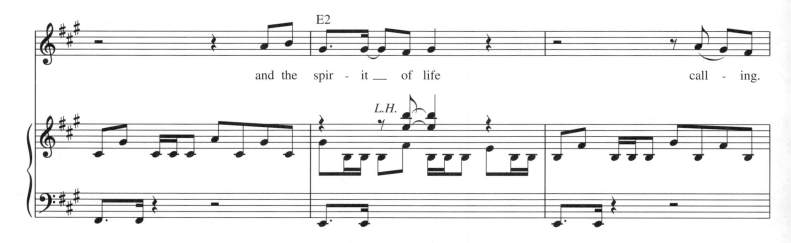

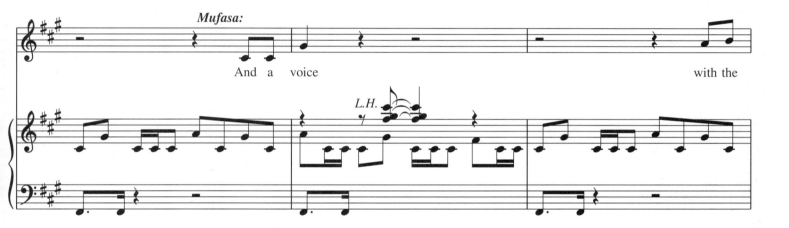

Chorus:
Ma-me - la ma-me-la iyo. He - la.

Mufasa:
Wait, there's no moun-tain too great.

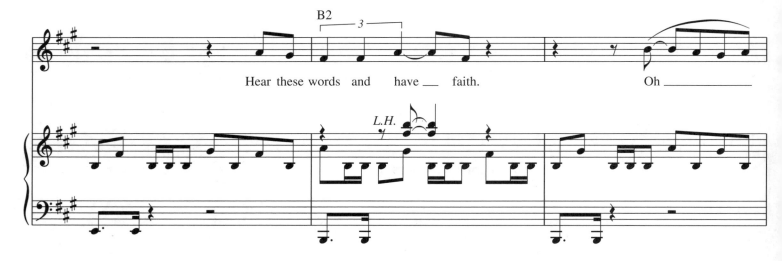

Hear these words and have __ faith. Oh _____

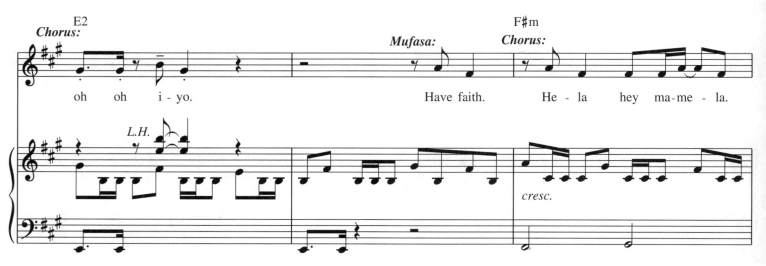

Chorus:
oh oh i - yo.

Mufasa:
Have faith.

Chorus:
He - la hey ma-me - la.

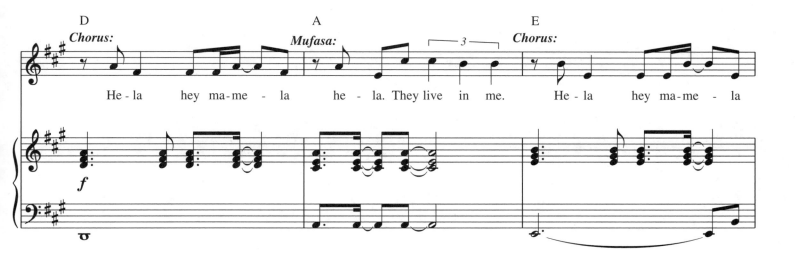

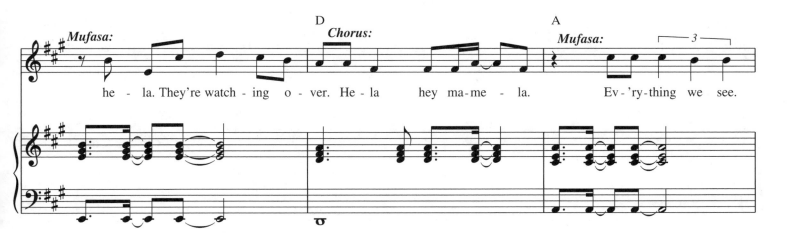

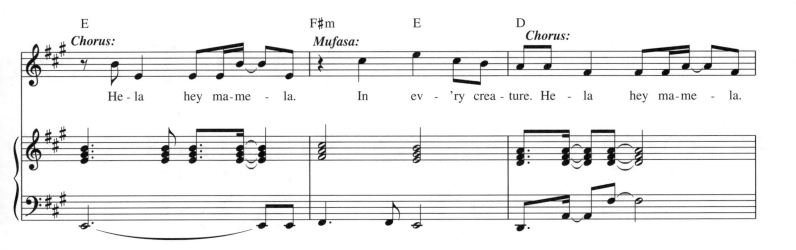

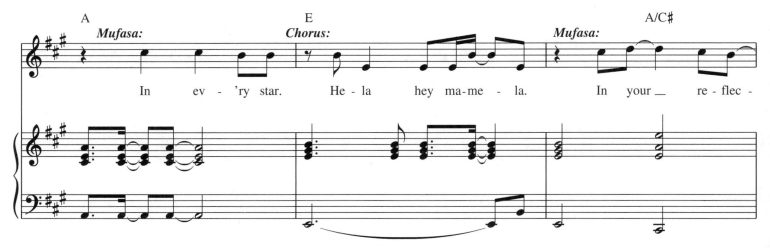

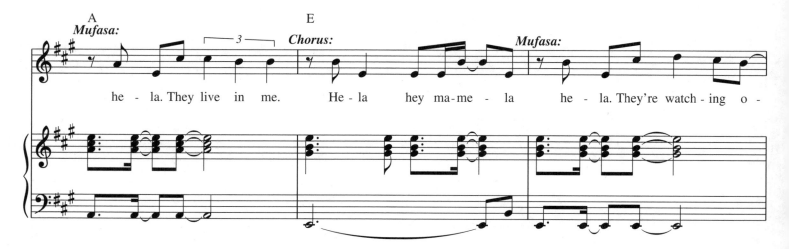

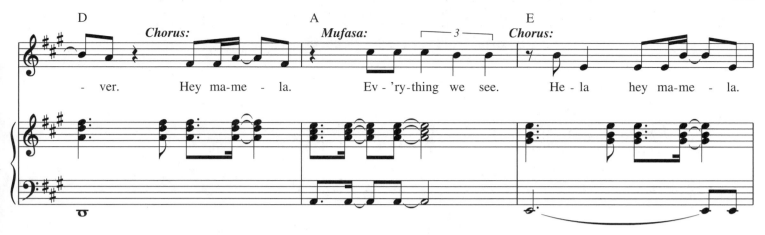

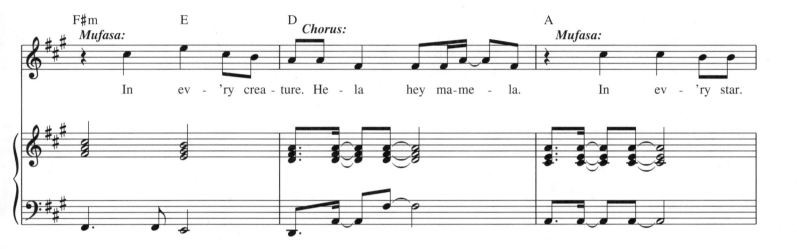

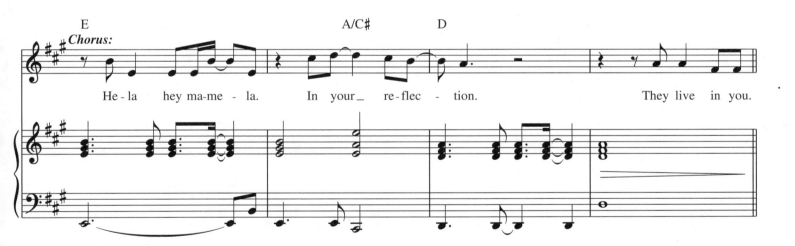

THE TIME OF YOUR LIFE
from Walt Disney's A BUG'S LIFE

Words and Music by
RANDY NEWMAN

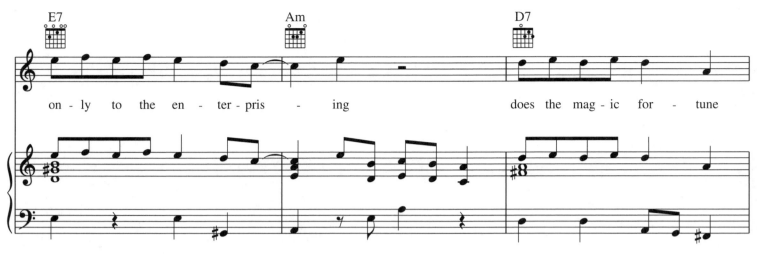

on - ly to the en - ter - pris - ing does the mag - ic for - tune

cook - ie go. Be - lieve me, it's the time _____ of your life,

so live it well. ___ It's the time _

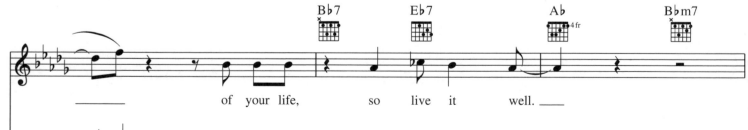

_____ of your life, so live it well. ___

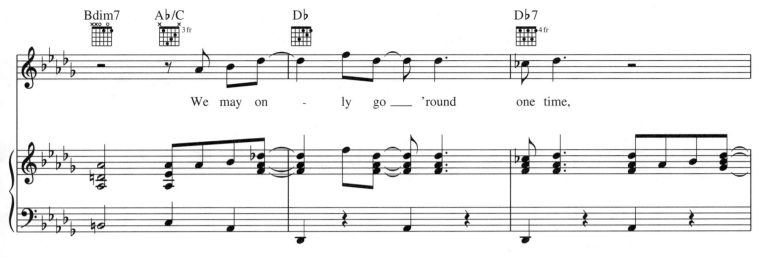

We may on - ly go ____ 'round one time,

as far as I can tell. It's the time _____ of your life, _

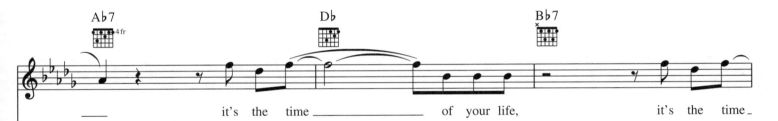

____ it's the time _____ of your life, it's the time_

_____ of your life so live it well.

TRUE LOVE'S KISS
from Walt Disney Pictures' ENCHANTED

Music by ALAN MENKEN
Lyrics by STEPHEN SCHWARTZ

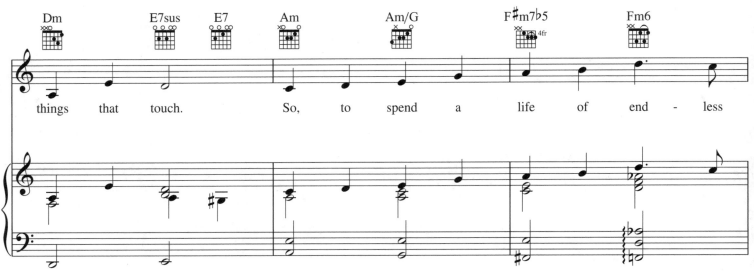

things that touch.　So, to spend a life of end - less

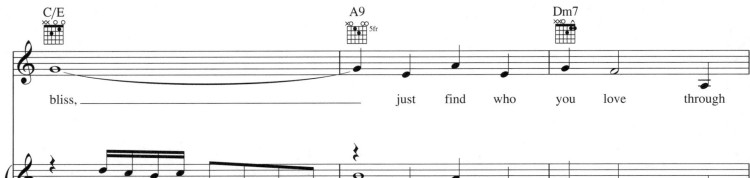

bliss, ＿＿＿＿＿＿＿＿＿＿ just find who you love through

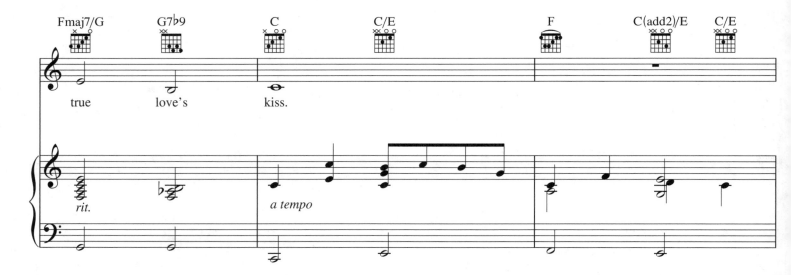

true love's kiss.

rit.　*a tempo*

Light Waltz, in one

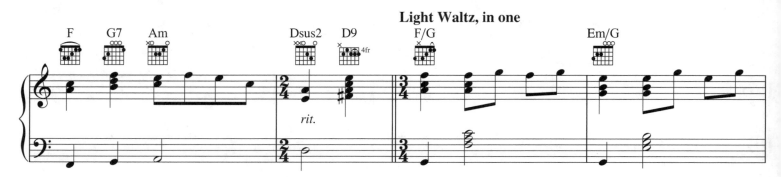

rit.

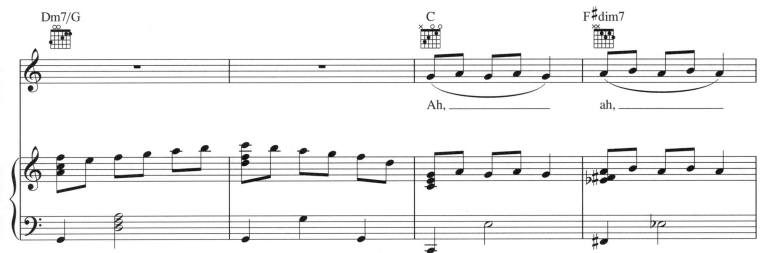

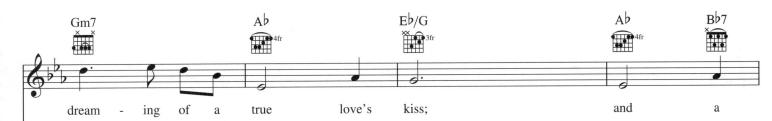

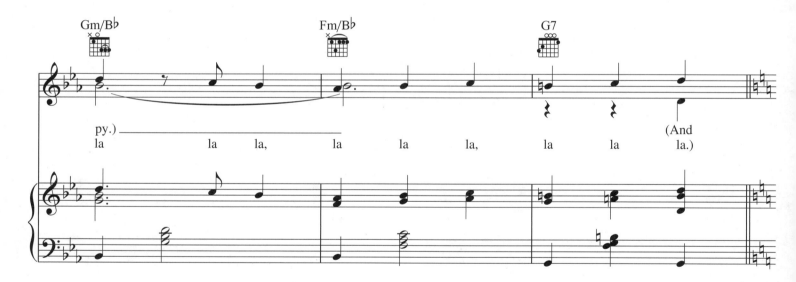

TWO WORLDS

from Walt Disney Pictures' TARZAN™

Words and Music by
PHIL COLLINS

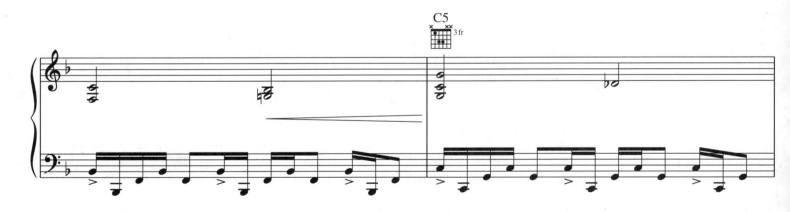

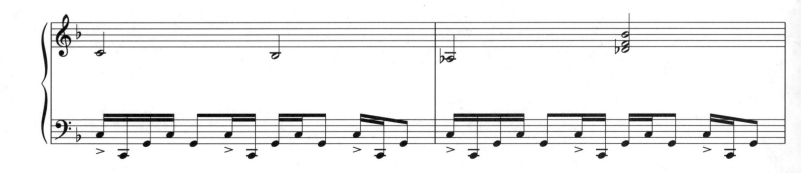

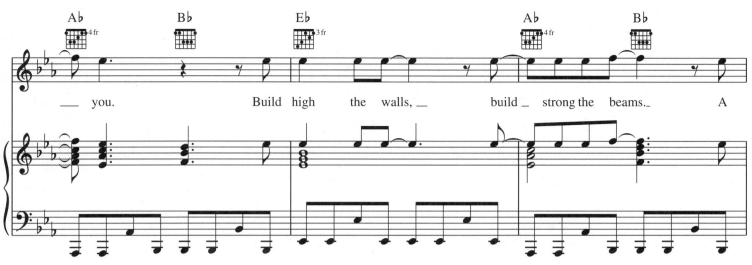

you. Build high the walls, __ build __ strong the beams.__ A

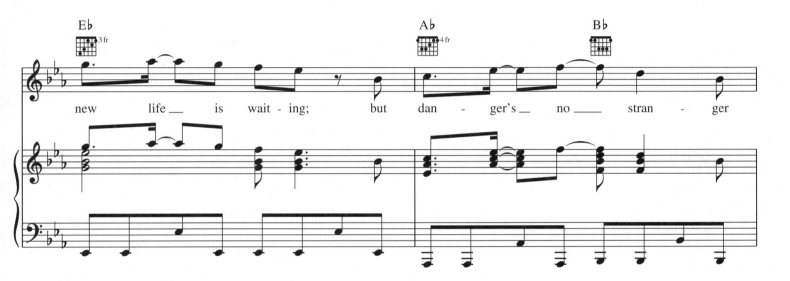

new life __ is wait-ing; but dan - ger's __ no __ stran - ger

here.

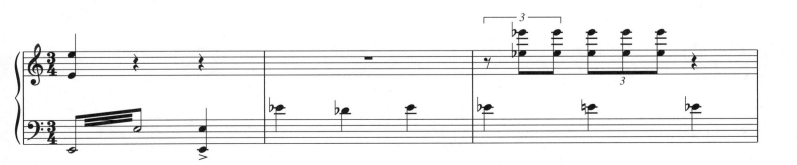

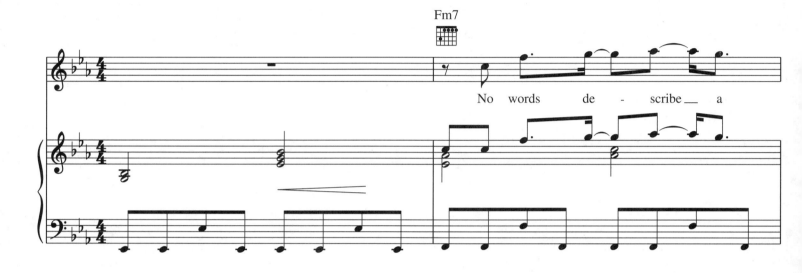

No words de - scribe___ a moth-er's tears.

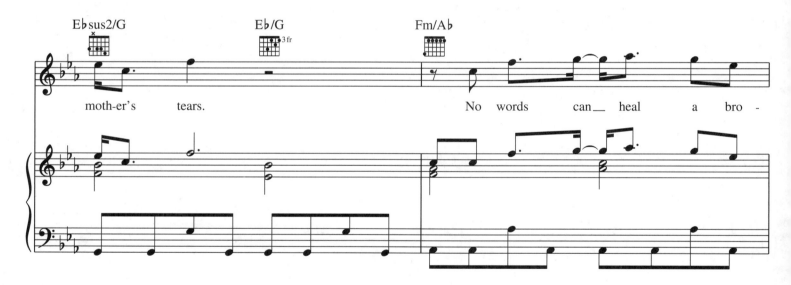

No words can___ heal a bro - ken heart.

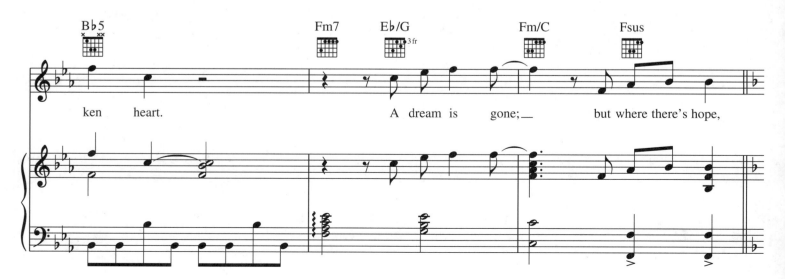

A dream is gone;___ but where there's hope,

some - where,__ some-thing is call - ing__ for__ you. Two worlds,__ one

fam - i - ly. __ Trust your__ heart,__ let fate de - cide __ to

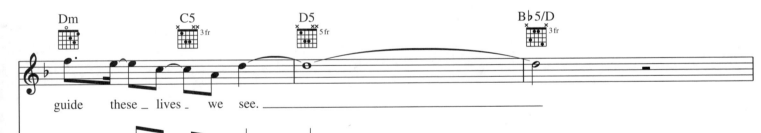

guide these __ lives __ we see. _____

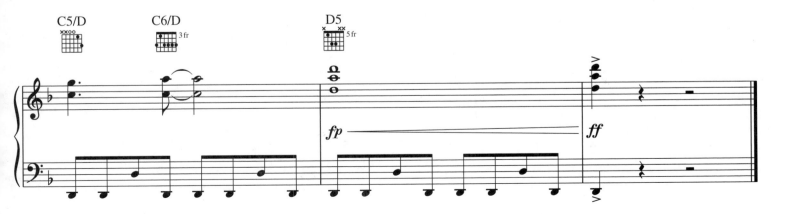

UNDER THE SEA
from Walt Disney's THE LITTLE MERMAID

Music by ALAN MENKEN
Lyrics by HOWARD ASHMAN

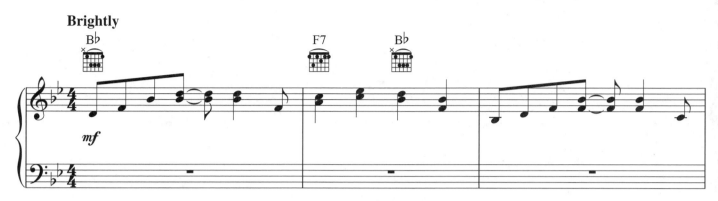

The sea - weed is al - ways green - er
Down here ___ all the fish is hap - py

in some - bod - y else - 's lake.   You dream ___ a - bout
as off ___ through the waves dey roll.   The fish ___ on the

go - ing up there. But that ___ is a big mis - take.
land ain't hap - py. They sad ___ 'cause they in the bowl.

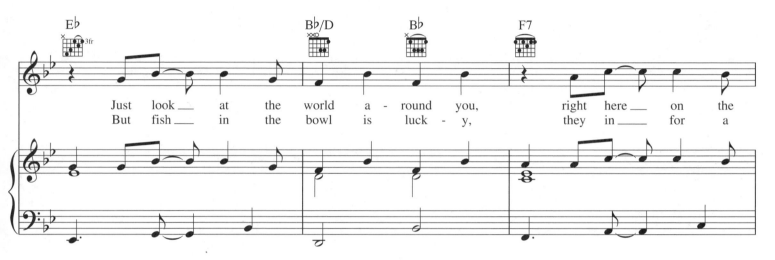

Just look ___ at the world a - round you, right here ___ on the
But fish ___ in the bowl is luck - y, they in ___ for a

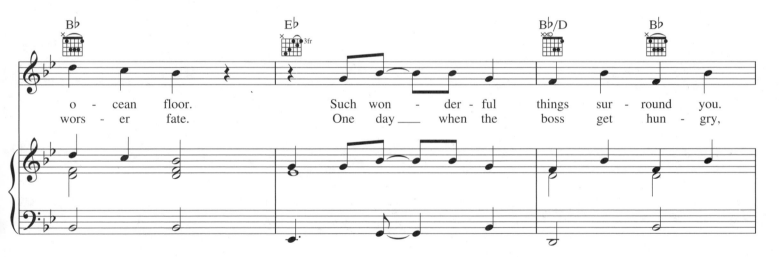

o - cean floor. Such won - der - ful things sur - round you.
wors - er fate. One day ___ when the boss get hun - gry,

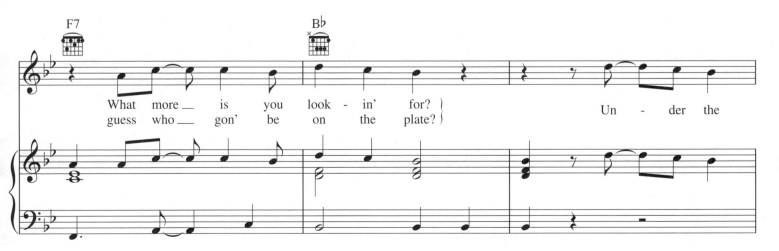

What more ___ is you look - in' for? Un - der the
guess who ___ gon' be on the plate?

sea, un - der the sea.

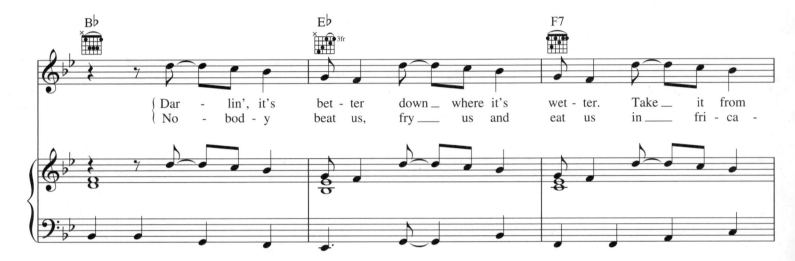

Dar - lin', it's bet - ter down __ where it's wet - ter. Take __ it from
No - bod - y beat us, fry __ us and eat us in __ fri - ca -

me. Up __ on the shore they work __ all day.
see. We __ what the land folks loves __ to cook.

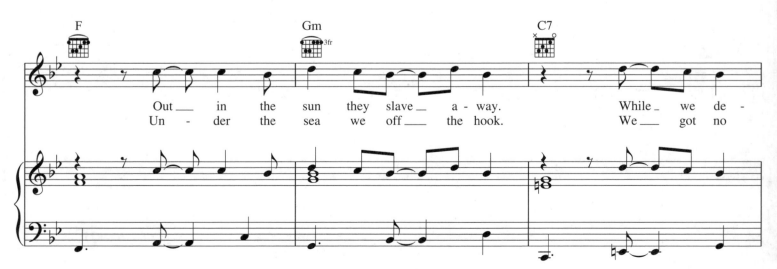

Out __ in the sun they slave __ a - way. While __ we de -
Un - der the sea we off __ the hook. We __ got no

vot - in' full - time to float - in' un - der the sea.
trou - bles, life ___ is the bub - bles un - der the

sea. Un - der the sea.

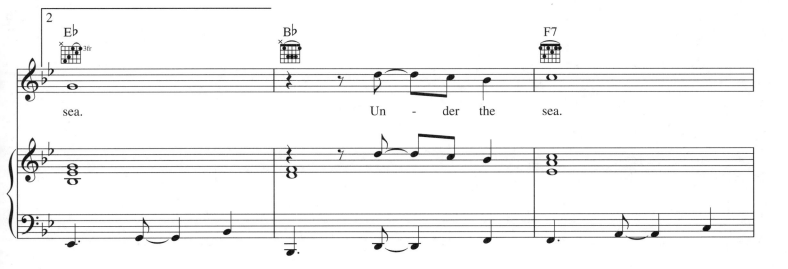

Since ___ life is sweet here we ___ got the beat here nat - u - ral -

ly. E - ven the stur - geon an' ___ the ray

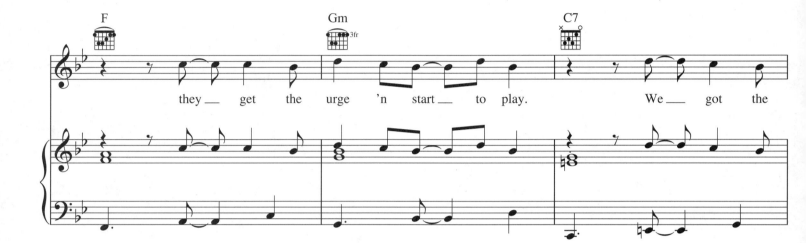

they ___ get the urge 'n start ___ to play. We ___ got the

spir - it, you ___ got to hear it un – der the sea.

The newt ___ play the flute. The carp ___ play the harp. The plaice ___

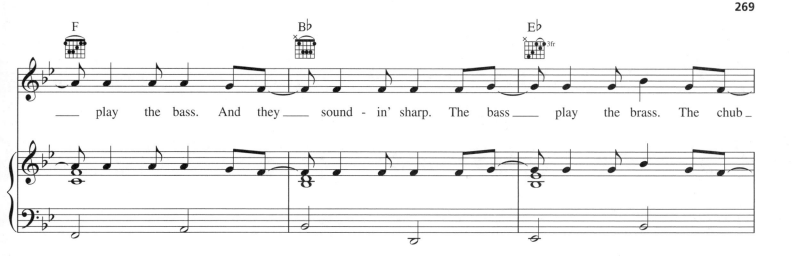

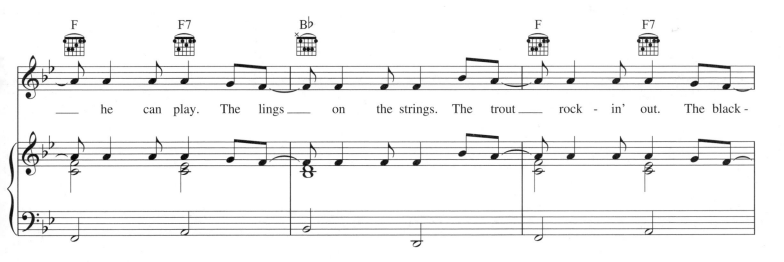

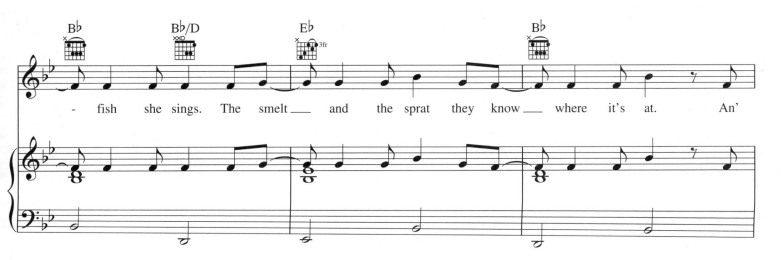

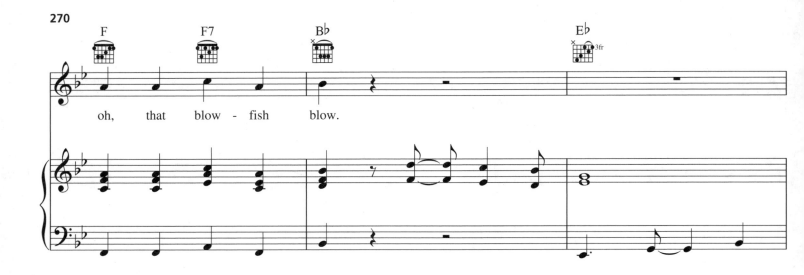

oh,   that   blow - fish   blow.

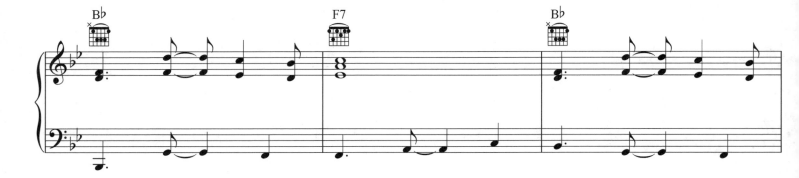

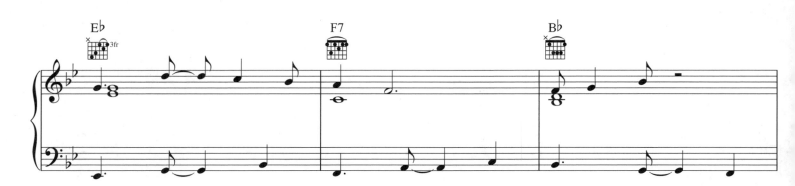

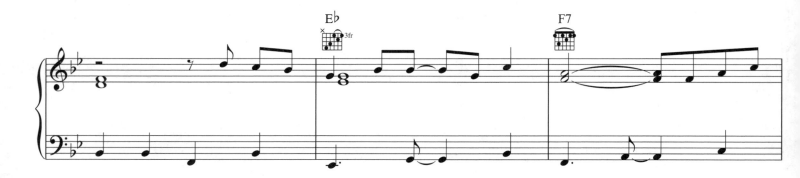

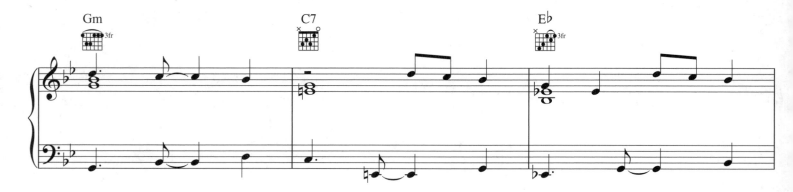

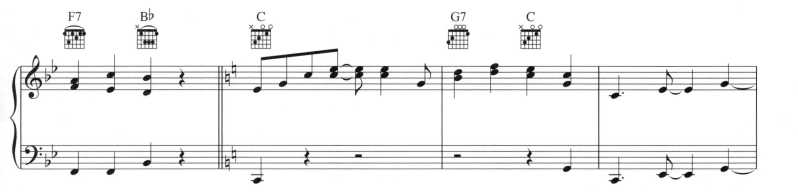

Un - der the   sea.   Un - der the   sea.

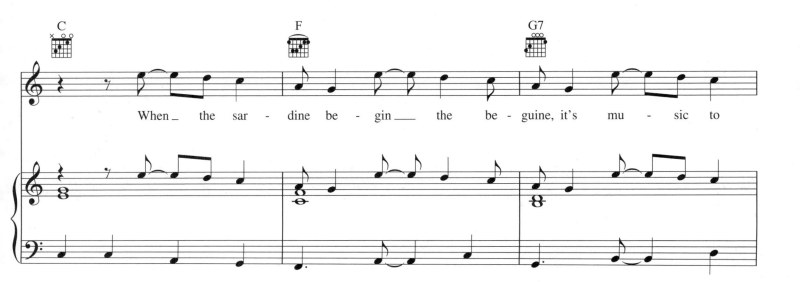

When _ the sar - dine be - gin __ the be - guine, it's mu - sic to

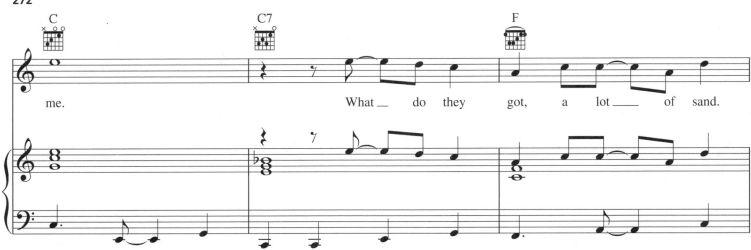

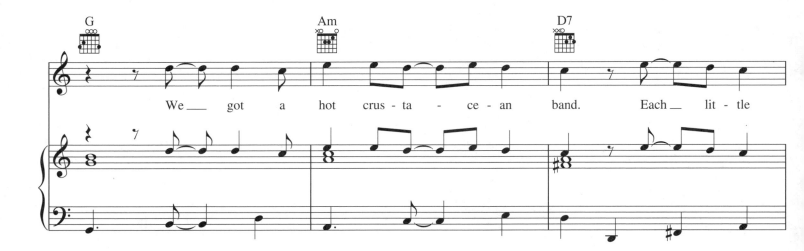

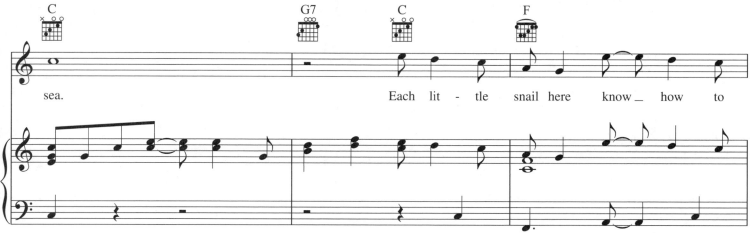

sea. Each lit-tle snail here know_ how to

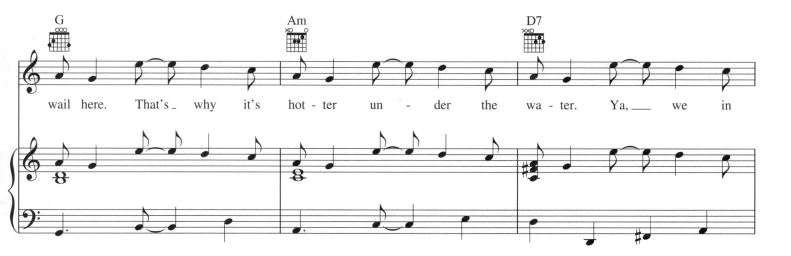

wail here. That's_ why it's hot-ter un-der the wa-ter. Ya,_ we in

luck here down_ in the muck here un-der the sea.__

WE'RE ALL IN THIS TOGETHER

from the Disney Channel Original Movie HIGH SCHOOL MUSICAL

Words and Music by MATTHEW GERRARD
and ROBBIE NEVIL

*Recorded a half step lower.

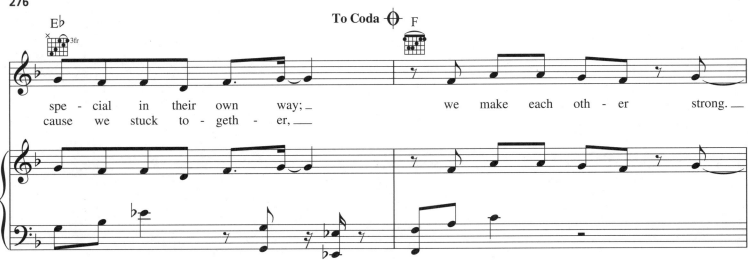

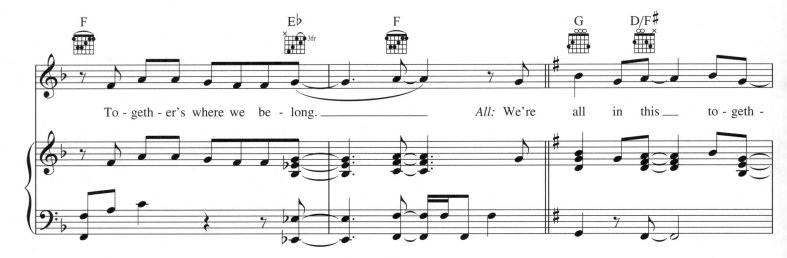

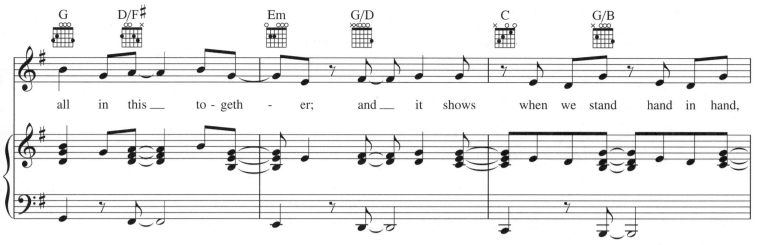

all in this __ to - geth - er; and __ it shows when we stand hand in hand,

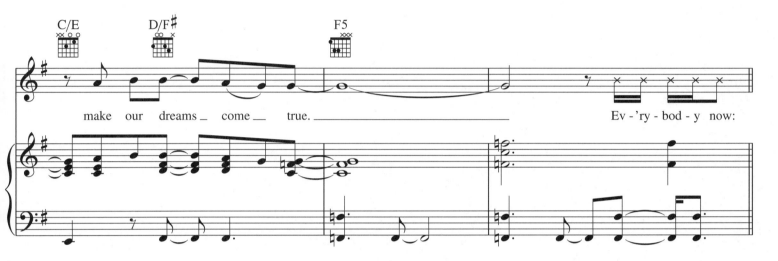

make our dreams __ come __ true. _____ Ev -'ry - bod - y now:

To - geth - er, to - geth - er, to - geth - er, ev -'ry - one.
To - geth - er, we're there __ for each oth - er ev -'ry time.

To - geth - er, to - geth - er, c' - mon, __ let's have some fun.
To - geth - er, to - geth - er,

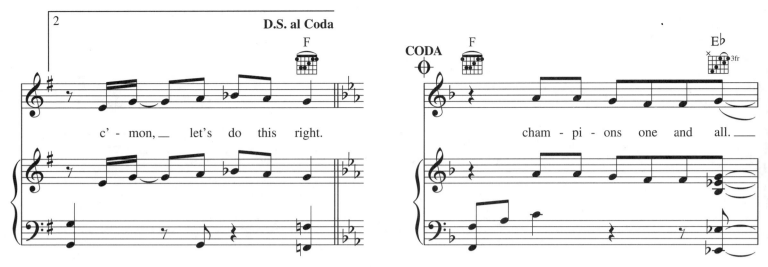

and we take ___ it. Wild cats, sing a - long; ___

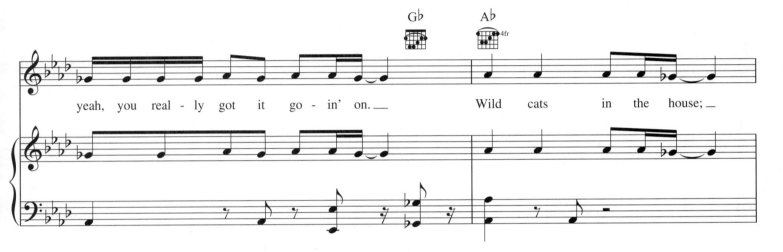

yeah, you real - ly got it go - in' on. ___ Wild cats in the house; ___

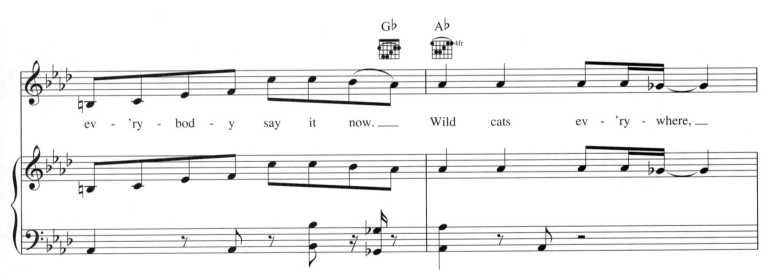

ev - 'ry - bod - y say it now. ___ Wild cats ev - 'ry - where, ___

wave your hands up in the air. ___ That's the way we do it; let's get

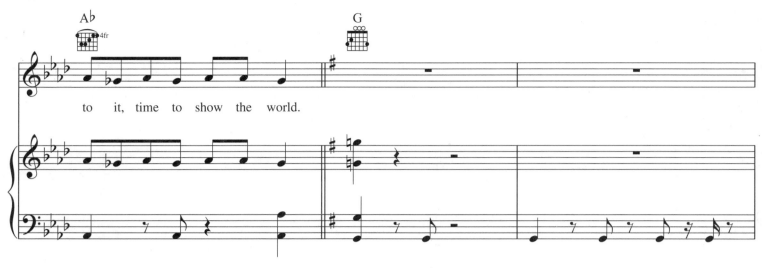

to it, time to show the world.

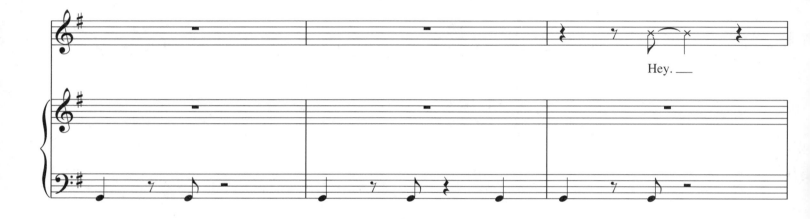

Hey. —

Oh. —   Hey, —   oh, ___   al - right, here we go. We're

all in this __ to - geth - er;   once __ we know   that we are, we're all stars,
all in this __ to - geth - er;   when __ we reach,   we can fly,   know in - side

and we see ___ that. We're all in this ___ to - geth - er; and ___ it shows
we can make ___ it. We're all in this ___ to - geth - er; once ___ we see

when we stand hand in hand, make our dreams ___ come... We're
there's a chance that we have,
and we take ___ it.

Wild cats ev - 'ry - where, ___ wave your hands up in the air. ___

That's the way we do it; let's get to it, c' - mon ___ ev - 'ry - one! ___

WHEN SHE LOVED ME

from Walt Disney Pictures' TOY STORY 2 - A Pixar Film

Music and Lyrics by
RANDY NEWMAN

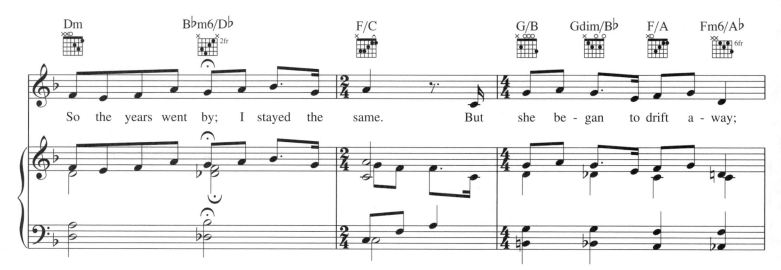

So the years went by; I stayed the same. But she be - gan to drift a - way;

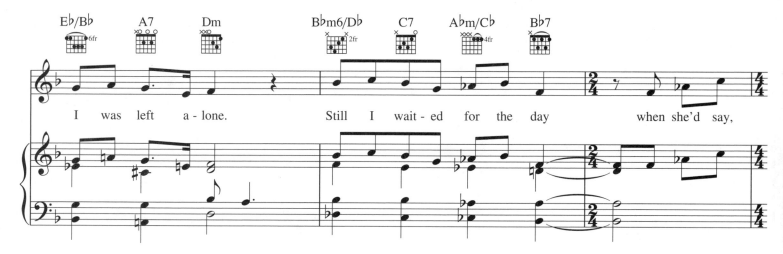

I was left a - lone. Still I wait - ed for the day when she'd say,

"I will al - ways love you." Lone - ly and for - got - ten,

rit.

a tempo

nev - er thought she'd look my way, and she smiled at me and held me just like she used to do, like she

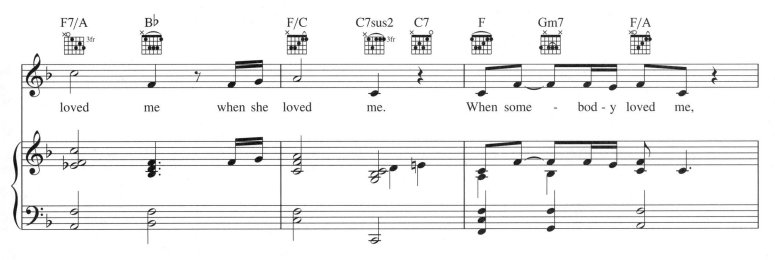

loved me when she loved me. When some - bod-y loved me,

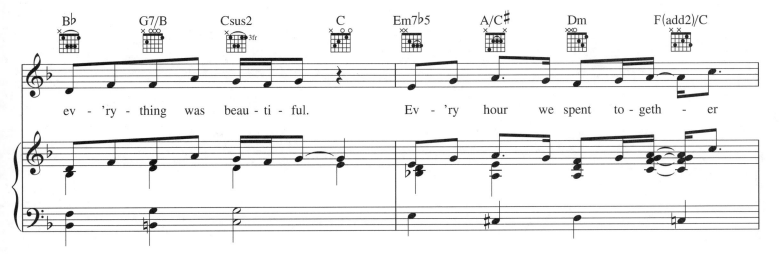

ev-'ry-thing was beau-ti-ful. Ev-'ry hour we spent to-geth - er

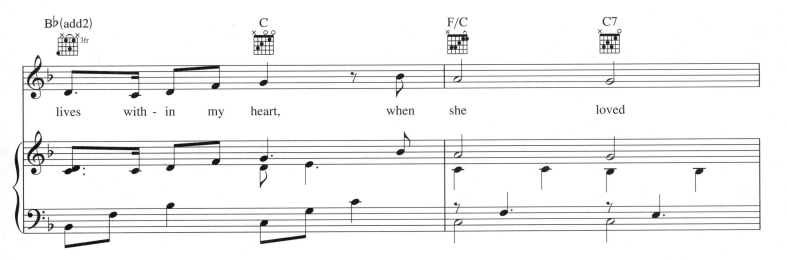

lives with - in my heart, when she loved

me.

A WHOLE NEW WORLD

from Walt Disney's ALADDIN

Music by ALAN MENKEN
Lyrics by TIM RICE

Sweetly

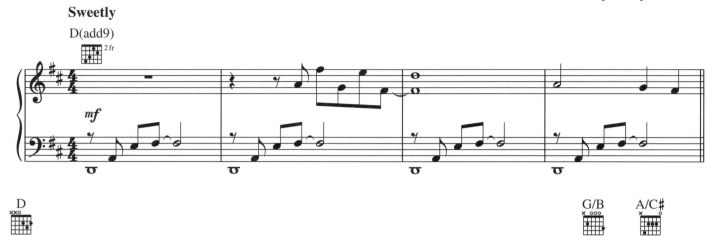

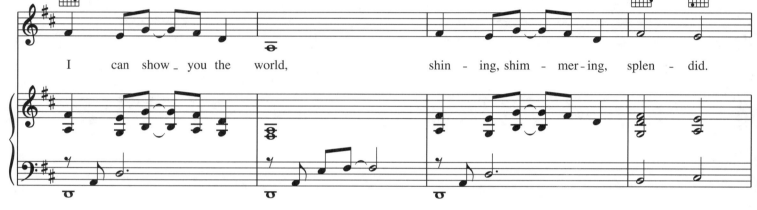

I can show you the world, shin-ing, shim-mer-ing, splen-did.

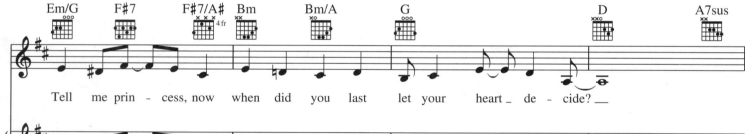

Tell me prin-cess, now when did you last let your heart de-cide?

I can o-pen your eyes take you won-der by won-der

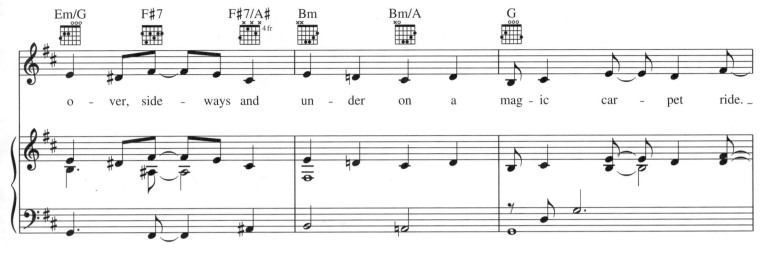

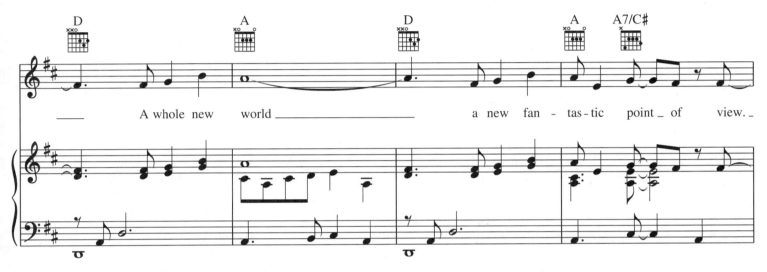

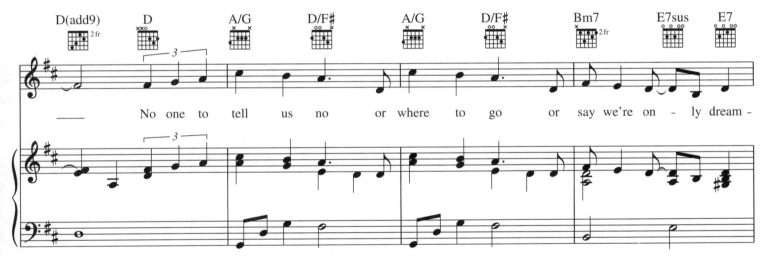

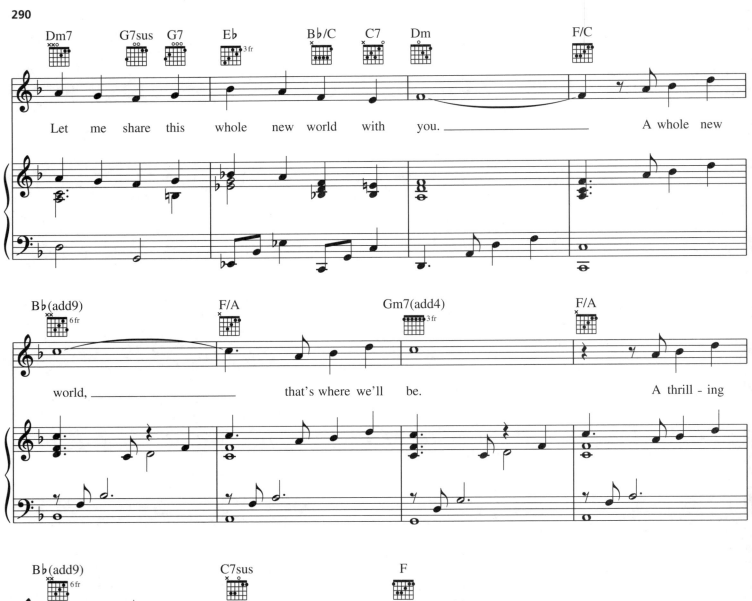

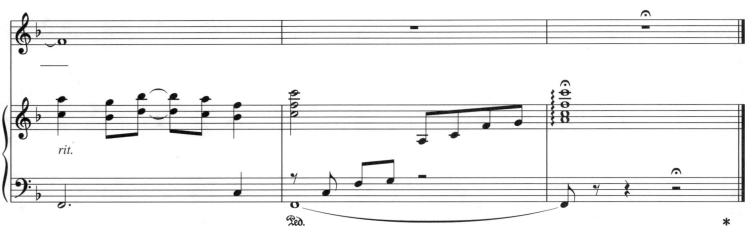

YOU ARE THE MUSIC IN ME

from the Disney Channel Original Movie HIGH SCHOOL MUSICAL 2

Words and Music by
JAMIE HOUSTON

Moderately fast Rock

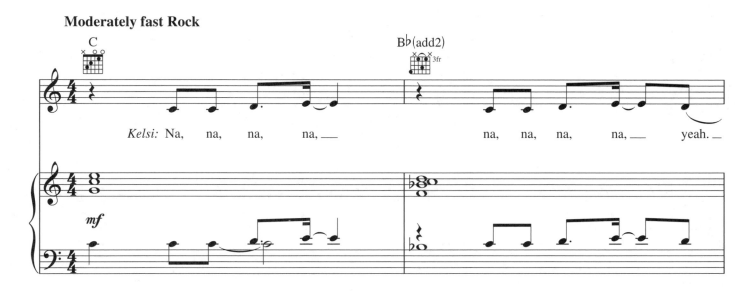

Kelsi: Na, na, na, na, ___ na, na, na, na, ___ yeah. ___

You are the mu-sic in me. ___

You know, the words, ___ "once up-on a time" make you lis-

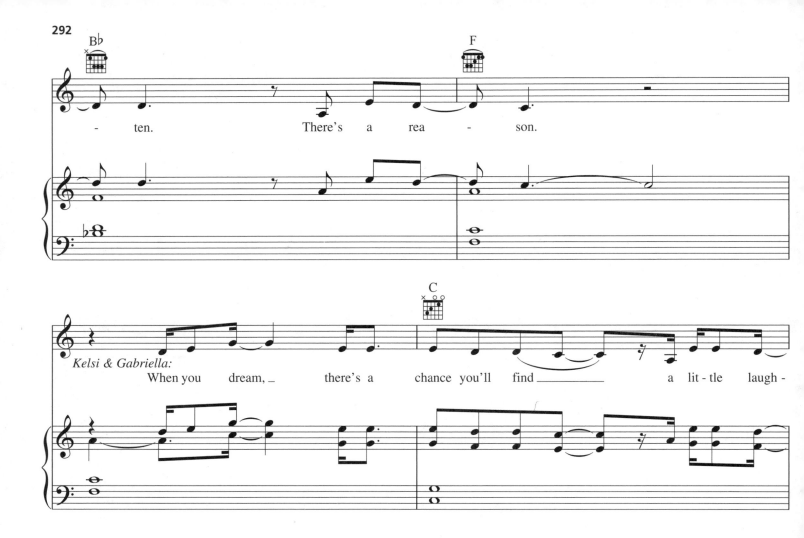

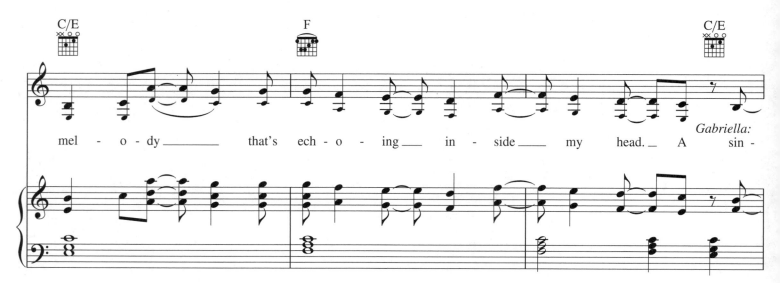

eas - y, be - cause you see the real me. As I *Both:* am you un -

- der - stand, and that's more than I've ev -

- er known. *Gabriella:* To hear your voice a - bove the noise, *Both:* and

know I'm not a - lone. *Gabriella:* Oh, you're sing - in' to me.

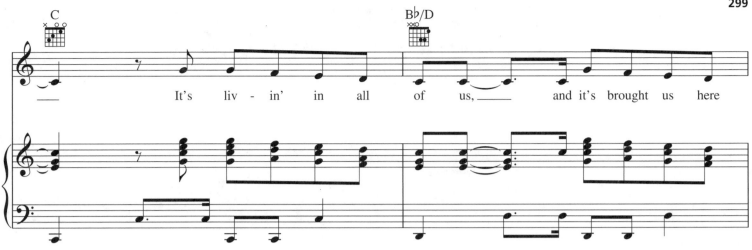

It's liv-in' in all of us, _____ and it's brought us here

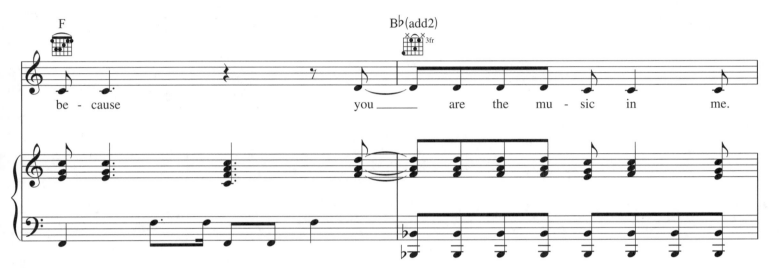

be - cause _____ you _____ are the mu - sic in me.

Na, na, na, na. Na, na, na, na, na. Na, na, na, na. You _____

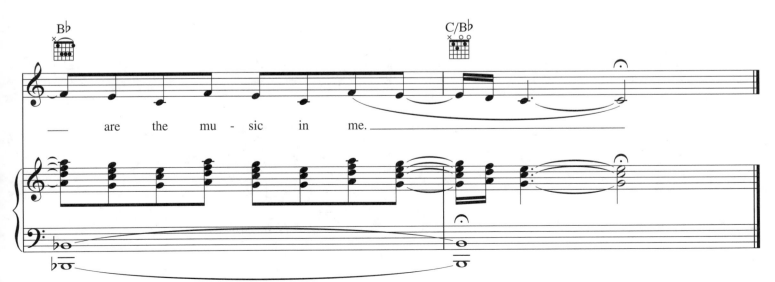

_____ are the mu - sic in me. _____

WOODY'S ROUNDUP
from Walt Disney Pictures' TOY STORY 2 – A Pixar Film

Music and Lyrics by
RANDY NEWMAN

Bright Two-beat

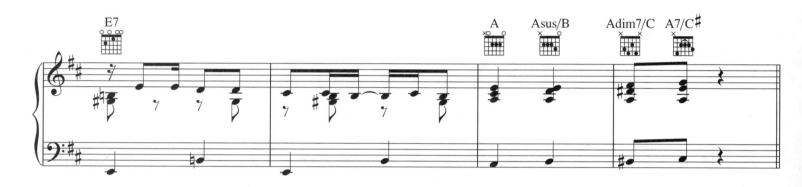

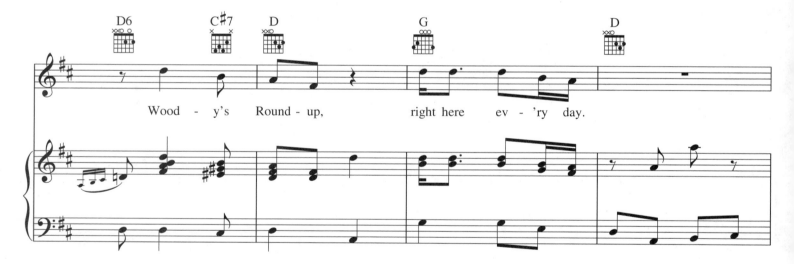

Wood - y's Round - up, right here ev - 'ry day.

Wood - y's Round - up, come on, it's time to play. There's

Jes - se, the yo - del - in' cow - girl. (O - dl lay - ee o - dl o ho o - dl

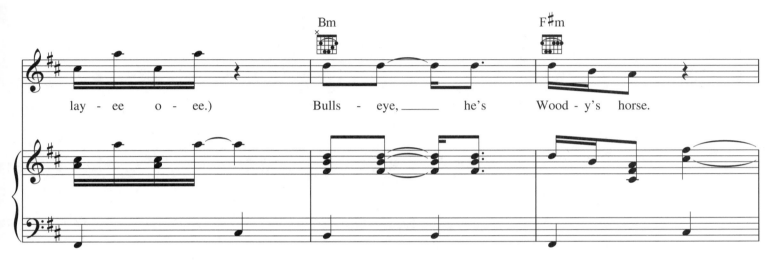

lay - ee o - ee.) Bulls - eye, _____ he's Wood - y's horse.

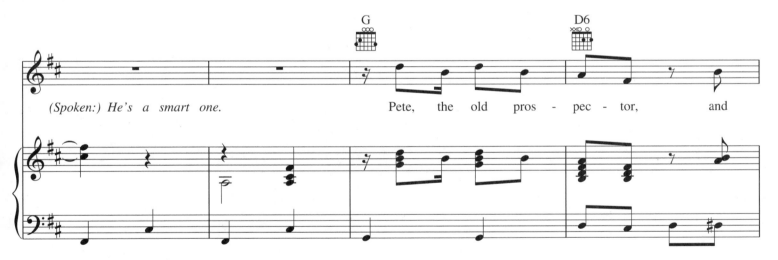

(Spoken:) He's a smart one. Pete, the old pros - pec - tor, and

Wood - y, the man him - self, of course. It's time for Wood - y's Round - up.

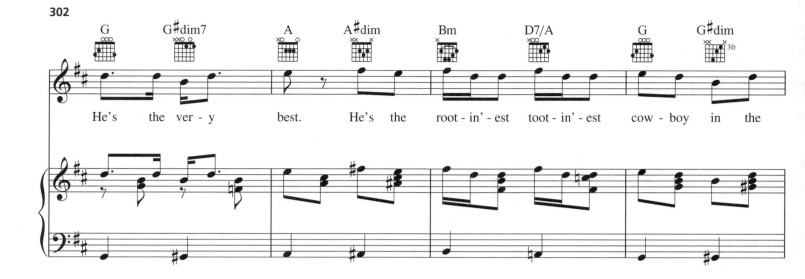

He's the ver - y best. He's the root - in' - est toot - in' - est cow - boy in the

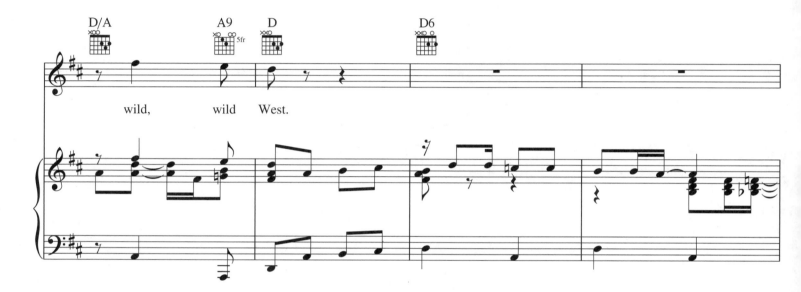

wild, wild West.

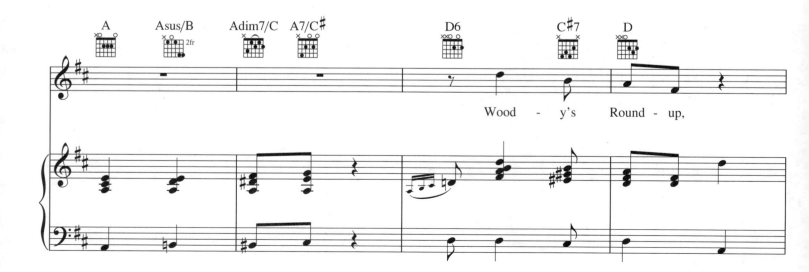

Wood - y's Round - up,

WRITTEN IN THE STARS

from Elton John and Tim Rice's AIDA

Music by ELTON JOHN
Lyrics by TIM RICE

To Coda

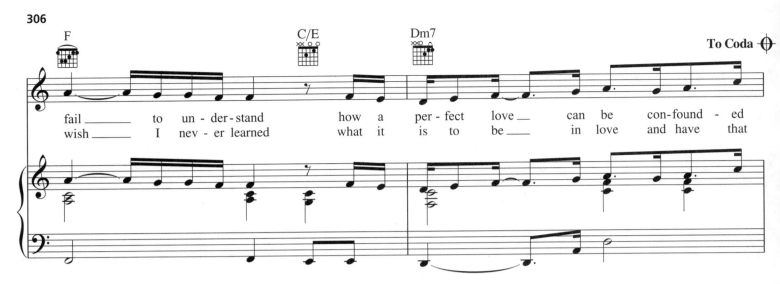

fail_____ to un-der-stand how a per-fect love ___ can be con-found -ed
wish_____ I nev - er learned what it is to be ___ in love and have that

out of hand._____ *Both:* Is it writ-ten in the stars? ___ Are we

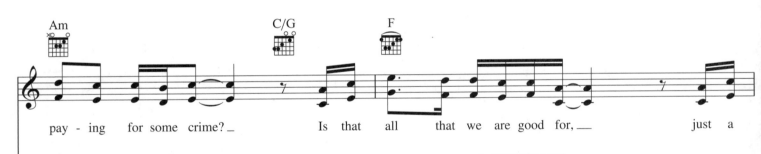

pay - ing for some crime? _ Is that all that we are good for, ___ just a

stretch of mor-tal time? _____ Is this God's ex - per - i - ment ____ in

which we have no say? In which we're giv-en par-a-dise, but

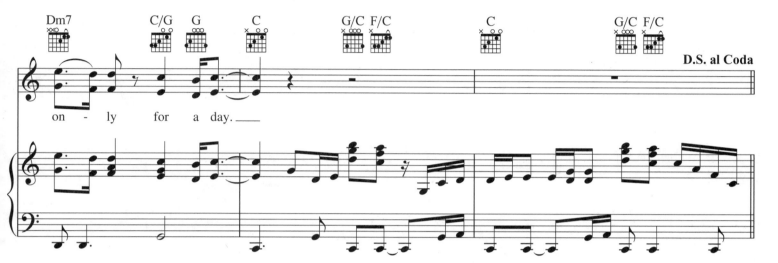

D.S. al Coda

on - ly for a day.

CODA

love re - turned. *Both:* Is it writ-ten in the stars? Are we
Oh

pay - ing for some crime? Is that all that we are good for, just a

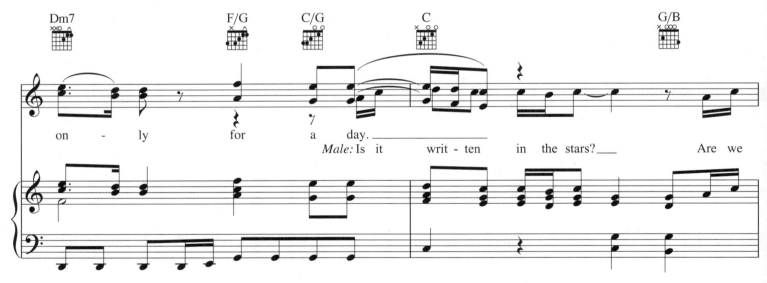

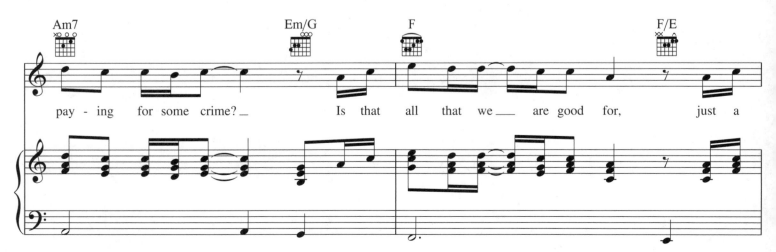

stretch of mor-tal time? ___ *Both:* Is ___ this God's ex - per - i - ment _____ *Male:* in

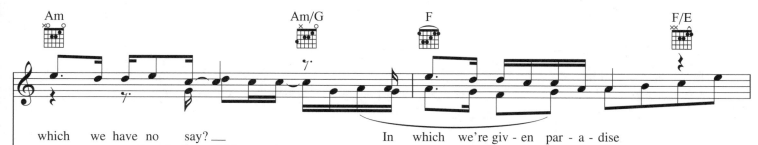

which we have no say? ___ In which we're giv - en par - a - dise
Female: In which we have ___ no say, _____ giv - en par - a -

on - ly *Both:* for a day. _____
dise _____

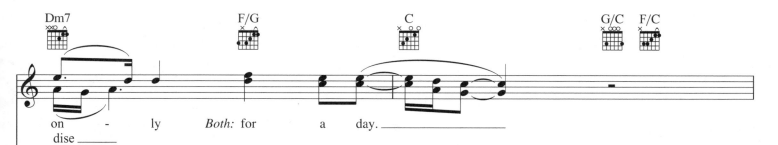

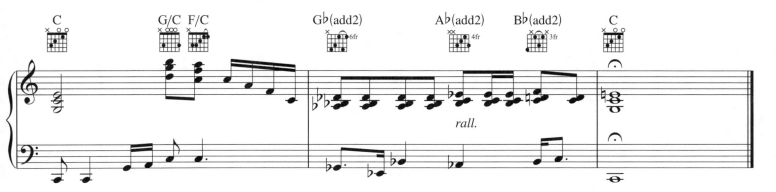

YOU'VE GOT A FRIEND IN ME

from Walt Disney's TOY STORY

Music and Lyrics by
RANDY NEWMAN

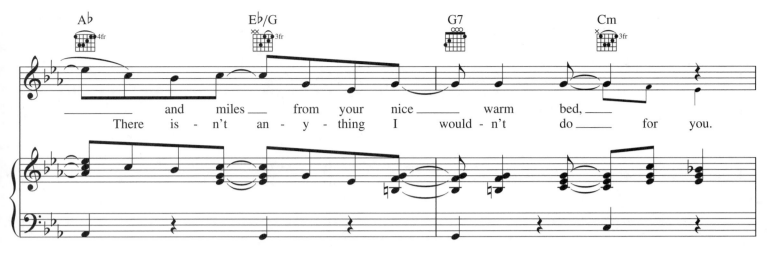

and miles ___ from your nice ___ warm bed, ___
There is - n't an - y - thing I would - n't do ___ for you.

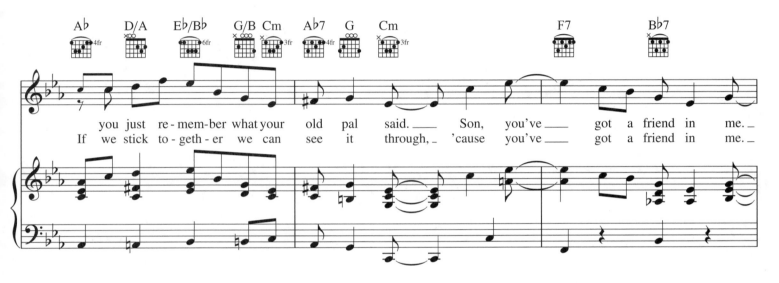

you just re - mem - ber what your old pal said. ___ Son, you've ___ got a friend in me. ___
If we stick to - geth - er we can see it through, _ 'cause you've ___ got a friend in me. ___

Yeah, you've ___ got a friend in me.
Yeah, you've ___ got a friend in me.

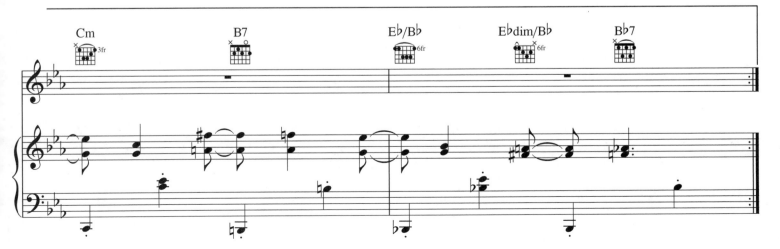

Now, some oth - er folks might be a lit - tle bit smart-er than I am,

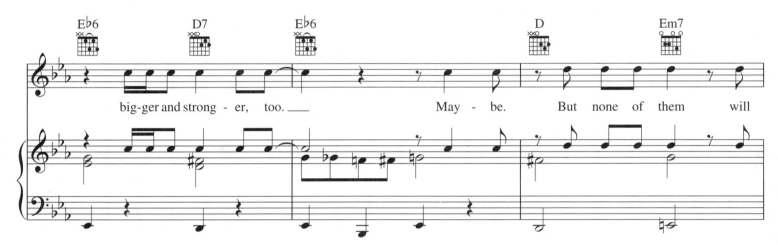

big-ger and strong - er, too. ___ May - be. But none of them will

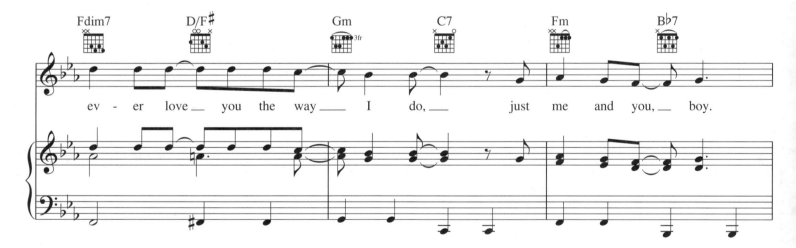

ev - er love ___ you the way ___ I do, ___ just me and you, ___ boy.

And as the years go by, ___ our friend - ship will nev - er die. __

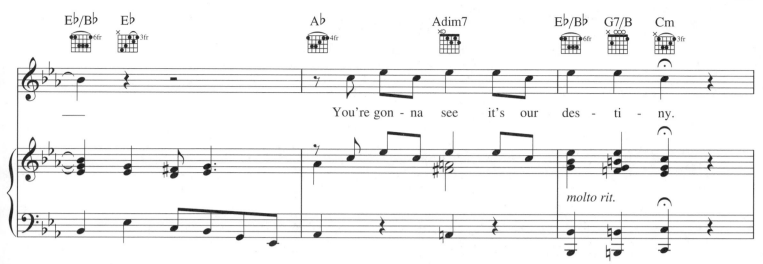

You're gon-na see it's our des-ti-ny.

molto rit.

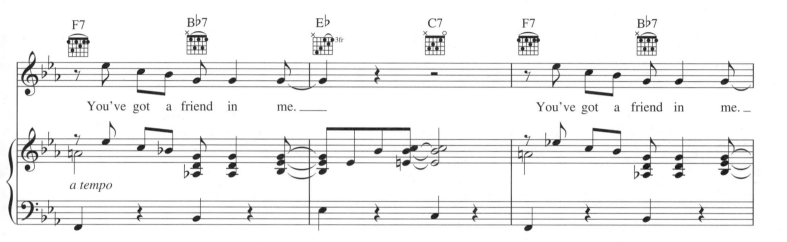

You've got a friend in me._____ You've got a friend in me.__

a tempo

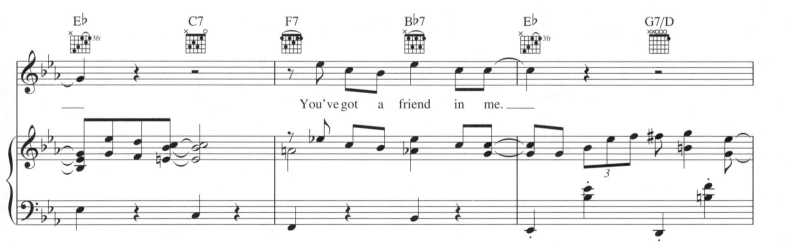

You've got a friend in me._____

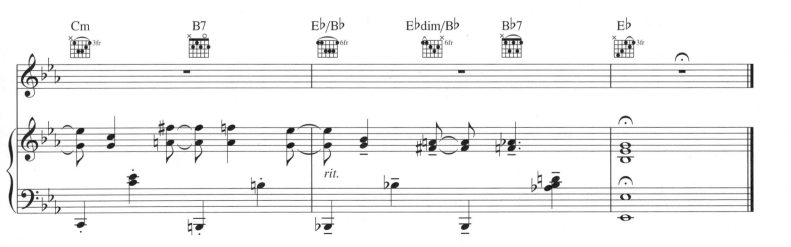

rit.

YOUR HEART WILL LEAD YOU HOME

from Walt Disney Pictures' THE TIGGER MOVIE

Words and Music by RICHARD M. SHERMAN,
ROBERT B. SHERMAN and KENNY LOGGINS

Recorded a half step lower.

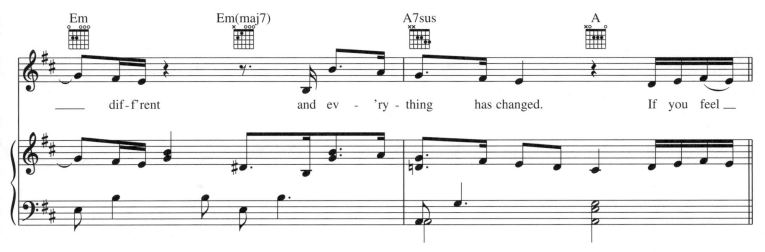

_____ dif-f'rent   and ev - 'ry - thing   has changed.   If you feel ___

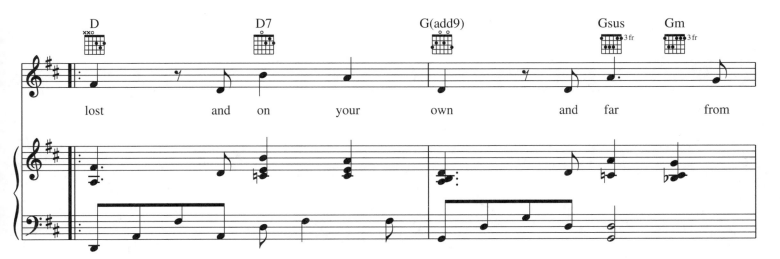

lost   and   on   your   own   and   far   from

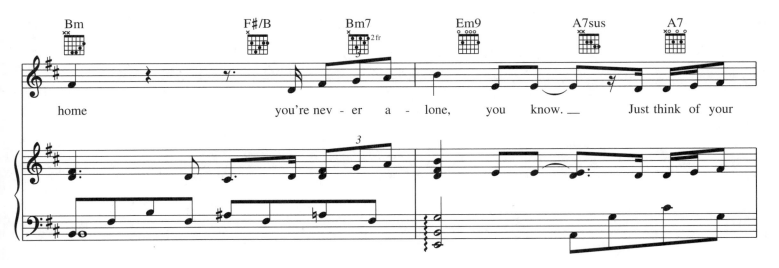

home   you're nev - er a - lone,   you   know. ___   Just think of your

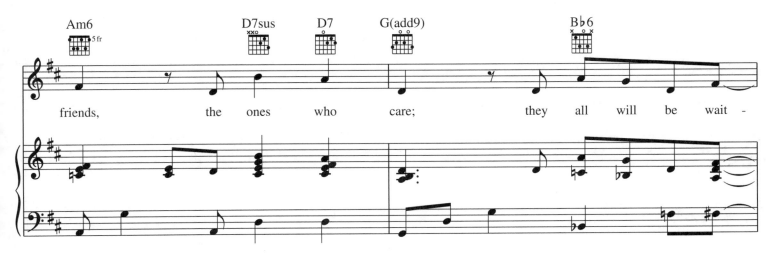

friends,   the   ones   who   care;   they   all   will   be   wait -

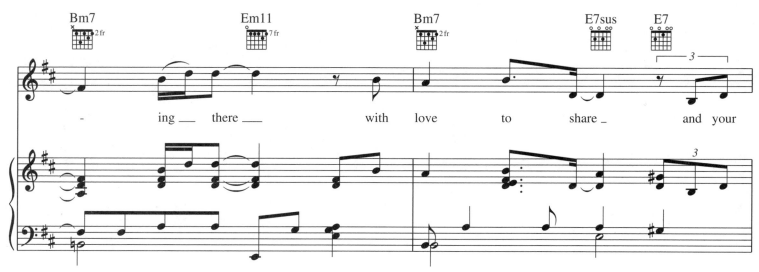

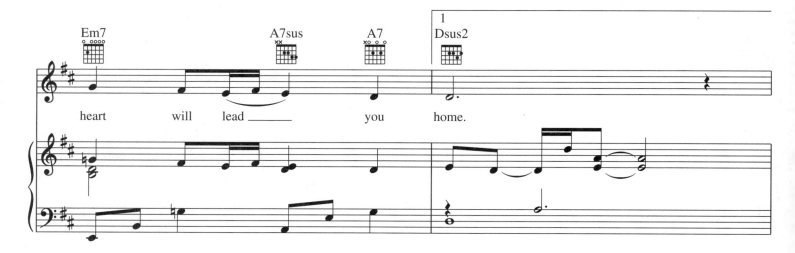

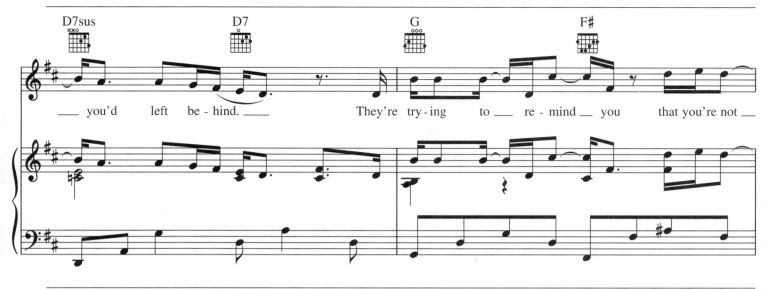

you'd left be-hind. They're try-ing to _re-mind_ you that you're not _

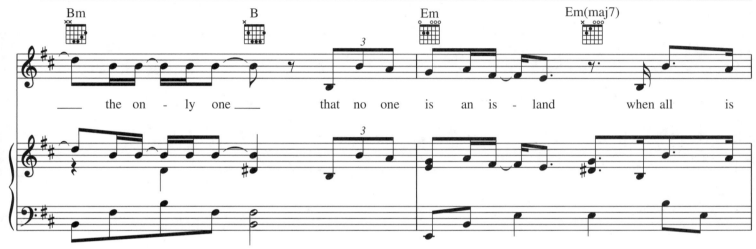

the on-ly one that no one is an is-land when all is

said and done. _ If you feel _ home.

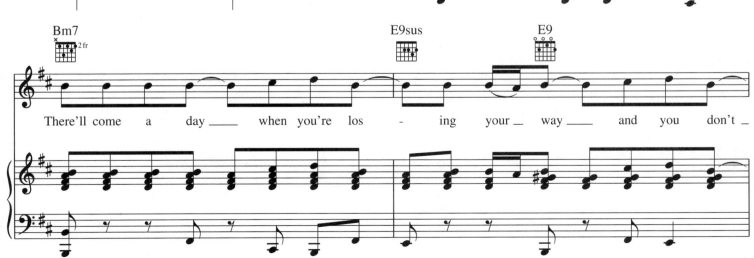

There'll come a day _ when you're los - ing your _ way _ and you don't _

home, you're nev - er a - lone, you know. _____ Just think of your

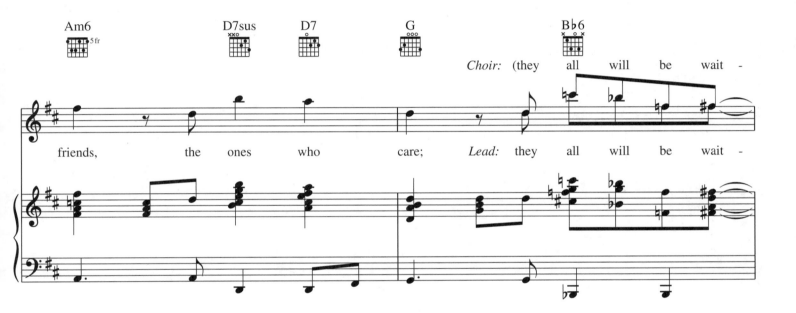

friends, the ones who care; *Lead:* they all will be wait -

Choir: (they all will be wait -

- ing there _____ with love to share. ___ And your

- ing there. _____

ZERO TO HERO
from Walt Disney Pictures' HERCULES

Music by ALAN MENKEN
Lyrics by DAVID ZIPPEL

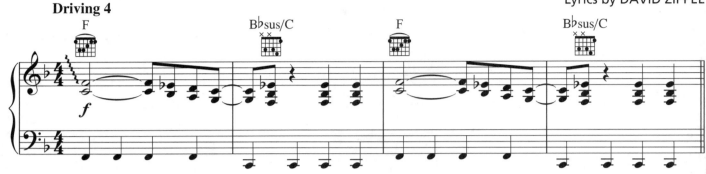

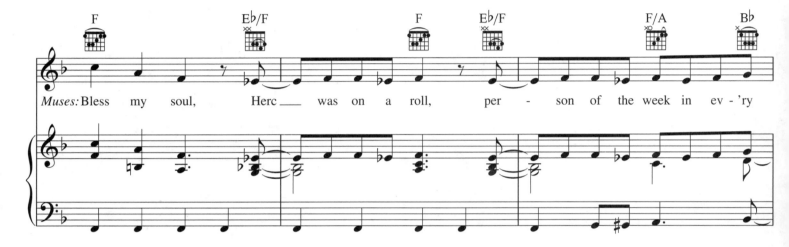

Muses: Bless my soul, Herc ___ was on a roll, per - son of the week in ev - 'ry

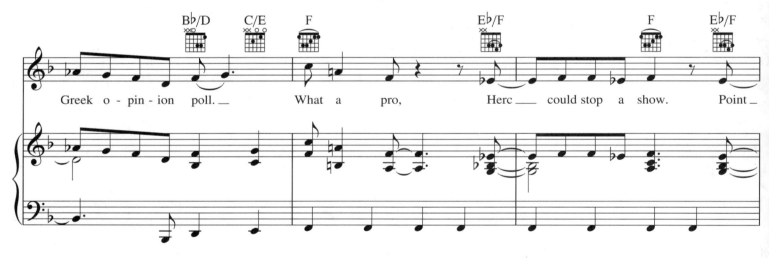

Greek o - pin - ion poll. ___ What a pro, Herc ___ could stop a show. Point ___

___ him at a mon - ster and you're talk - in' S. R. O. ___ He was a no ___ one, a

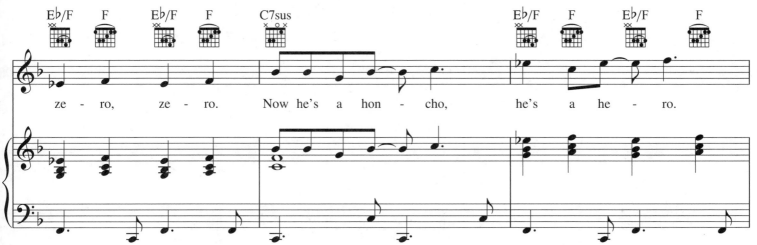

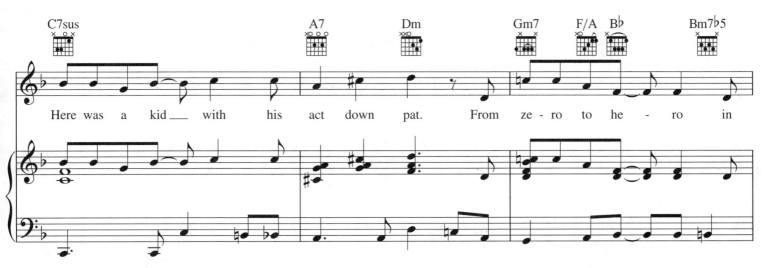

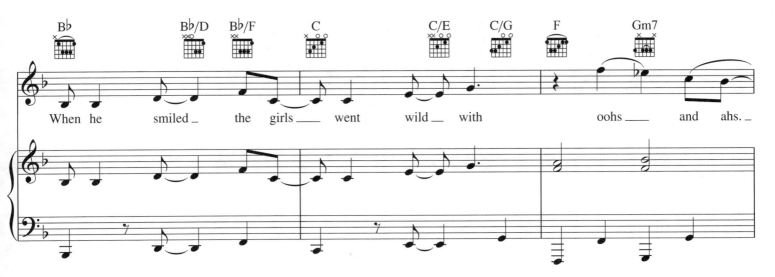

And they slapped his face __ on ev - 'ry vase. __ On

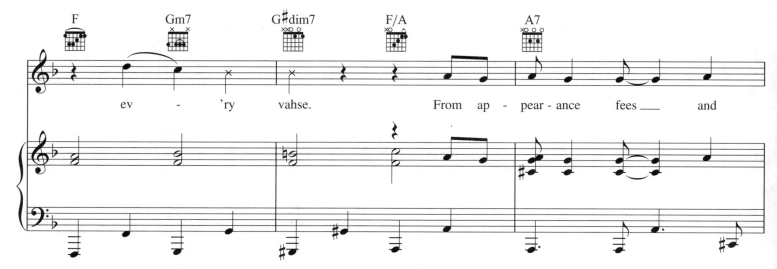

ev - 'ry vahse. From ap - pear - ance fees __ and

roy - al - ties __ our Herc had cash to burn. __ Now

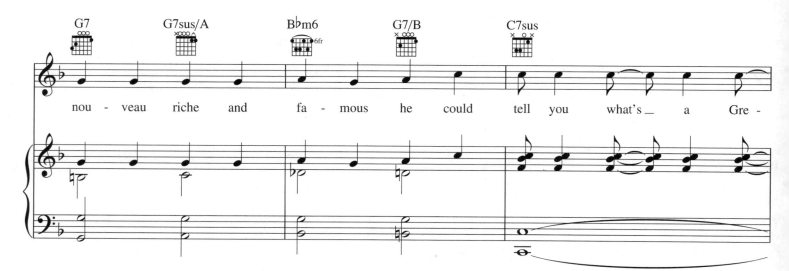

nou - veau riche and fa - mous he could tell you what's __ a Gre -

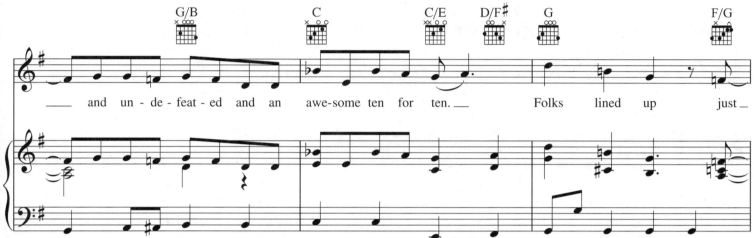

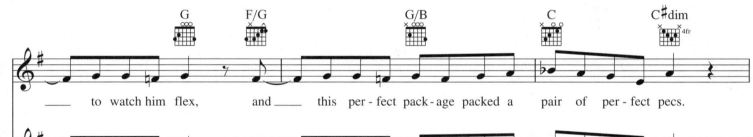

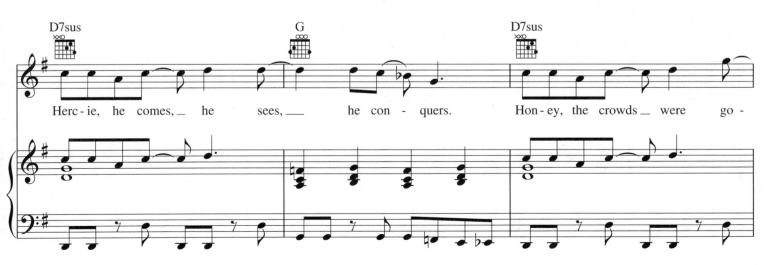

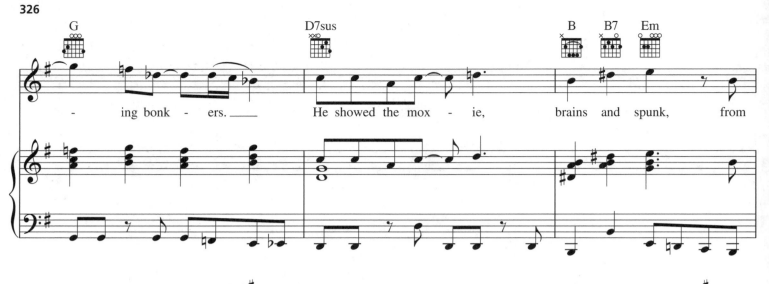

-ing bonk - ers. ___ He showed the mox - ie, brains and spunk, from

ze - ro to he - ro, a ma - jor ___ hunk. Ze - ro to he - ro and

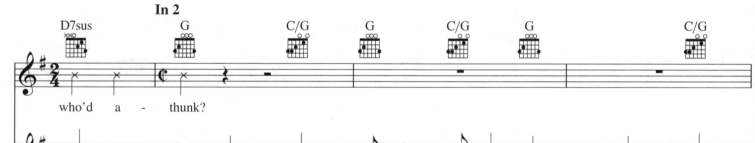

In 2

who'd a - thunk?

accel.

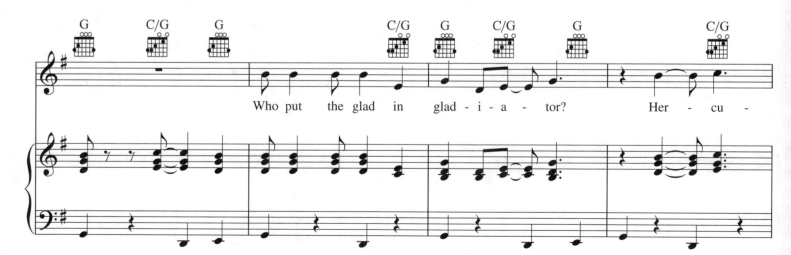

Who put the glad in glad - i - a - tor? Her - cu -

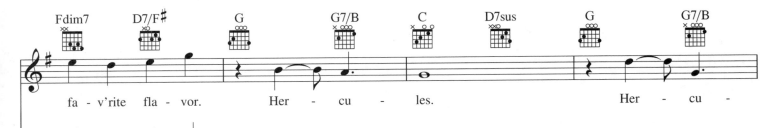

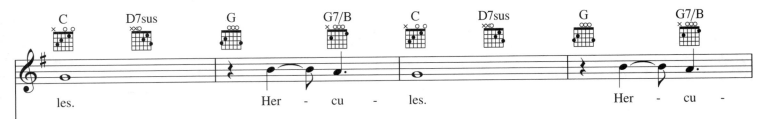

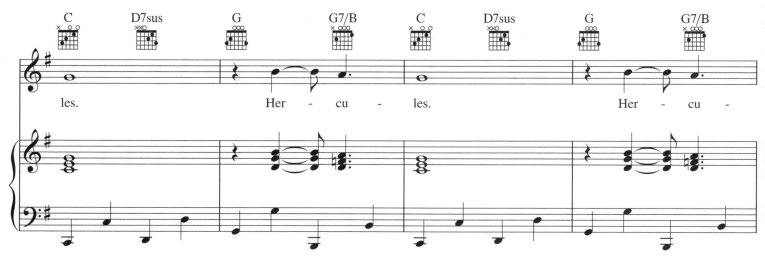

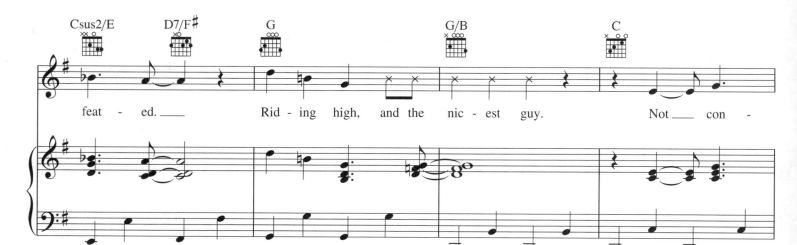

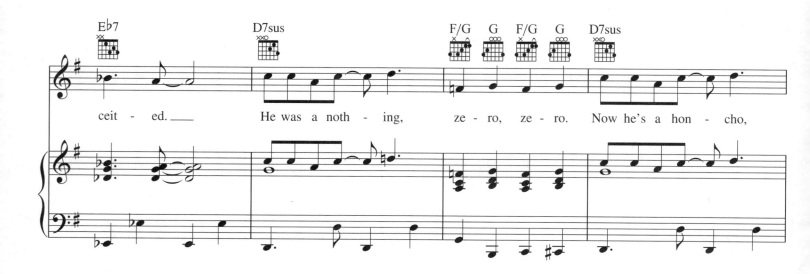

329

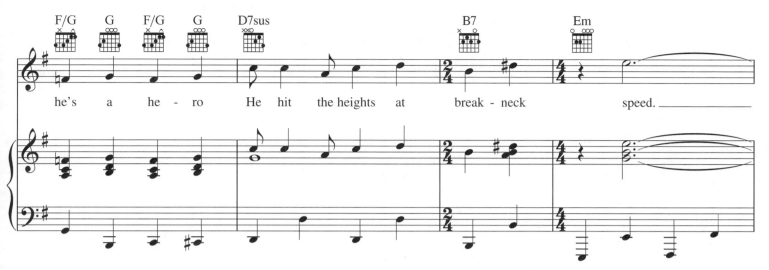

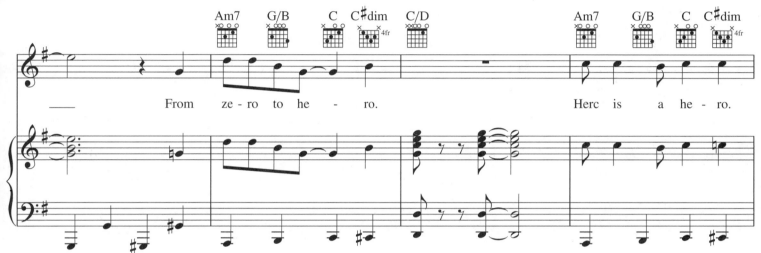

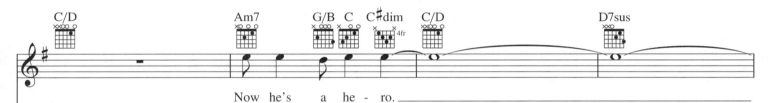

YOU'LL BE IN MY HEART
(Pop Version)
from Walt Disney Pictures' TARZAN™

Words and Music by
PHIL COLLINS

Come stop your cry - ing; _ it will be all right. Just take my hand,

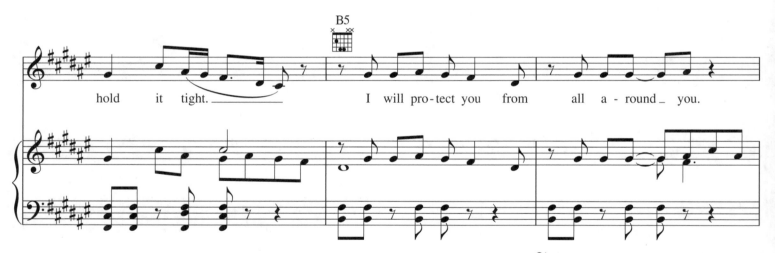

hold it tight. _____ I will pro-tect you from all a - round _ you.

I will be here; don't you _ cry.

For one so small you
Why can't they un - der-stand the

seem so ___ strong. ___ / way we ___ feel? ___
My arms will hold you, ___ keep you / They just don't trust _____ what they

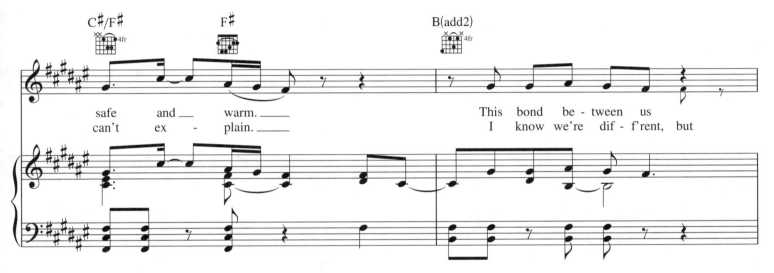

safe and ___ warm. _____ / can't ex - plain. _____
This bond be - tween us / I know we're dif - f'rent, but

can't be bro - ken. / deep in - side ___ us
I will be here; don't you ___ cry. / we're not that dif-fer-ent at all. _____
'Cause / And

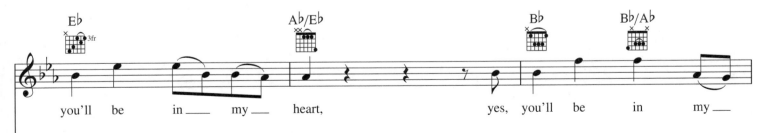

you'll be in ___ my ___ heart,
yes, you'll be in my ___

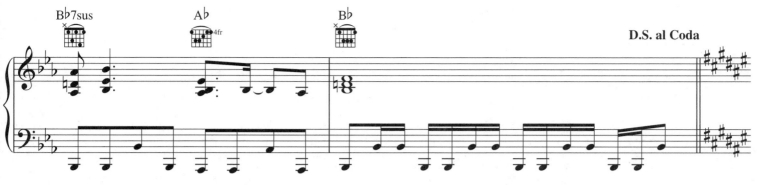

D.S. al Coda

CODA

Don't lis-ten to them, _____ 'cause you
des-ti-ny calls _ you, you

what do they _ know? _ We need each oth-er to
must _ be _ strong. _ I may not be with you, but you've

have, to _ hold. }
got to hold _ on. _ } They'll _ see _ in time, I _____

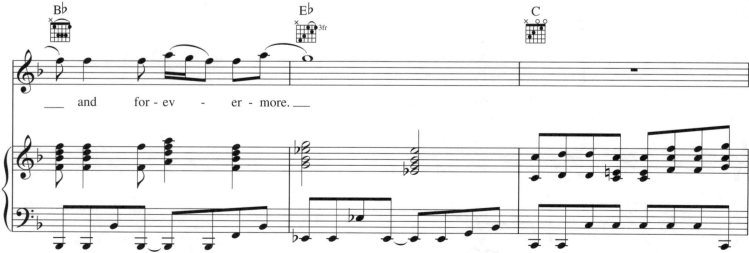

You'll be in _____ my ___ heart (You'll be here ___ in my heart.) ___ no mat- ter what ___ they ___

say. (I'll be with you.) You'll be here in _____ my ___ heart (I'll be there.) al-

- ways. Al - ways, _____

I'll be with you. I'll be